UNBROKEN

Embracing the Cracks that are Making You Whole

A 30-Day Bible Study for Women

RAYCHEL PERMAN

Published in the United States by RAYMA Team Media, a division of RAYMA Team, LLC.

2nd Edition

Paperback ISBN: 978-1-7366356-8-1

Cover Design by: Mandy Anderson

Cover Photo by: Raychel Perman

Back Cover Author Photo by: Lea Black

PRAISE FOR *UNBROKEN*

"As I work through the pages of this inspired study, I am finding that I am simultaneously brought to my knees AND lifted up. Raychel has a beautiful, accessible way of distilling the Truth and sharing with such tender transparency that I step away each day feeling - and knowing - that I am not alone and that the hope found in the cracks is a real, healing thing." **~Laura M.**

"When I contemplated doing the *UNBROKEN* Bible Study, I was terrified to touch some 'cracks' that I had tucked away for a very long time. Coach Raychel Chumley has made a difficult process step-by-step so that as I was dealing with my cracks and imperfections, I was also healing parts of them every day through Christ and reflection. Her words helped me embrace my cracks, work through them, and use them as a tool for a better tomorrow. Raychel connects with me because she too has been broken and she knows the pain I am experiencing. I have recommended this study to many of my friends and family and I would recommend it to any of you that would like to heal some of your own cracks." **~Bridget**

"*UNBROKEN* is a Bible Study where we, as women, can honestly share our brokenness and receive acceptance and Biblical wisdom." **~Sue G.**

"When I started this process of healing, I was BROKEN but am learning to understand that in healing and faith I can be UNBROKEN. My cracks tell my life story and while they will always remain a part of me, they will not define me and without this study I may never have come back to God the way I have." **~Kristin B.**

"*UNBROKEN* is a spectacular Bible Study. It has taught me that although I may have cracks in my life and be broken, there is hope! Although the process in healing the cracks may be long, Coach Raychel teaches us to embrace our cracks and face each day with new hope and truth! It has strengthened my faith and relationship with God and brought me new friendships with some wonderful women!" **~Melissa M.**

DEDICATION

To Mandy: Thank you for reminding me that my greatest healing comes from telling my story. Real. Always. Okay.

BY RAYCHEL PERMAN

She Cultivates Resilience

Truth Statement® Journals available at www.raymateammedia.com

WHAT TO EXPECT

During the next 30 days, you will explore stories of resilience and hope, along with examples from the Ancient Wisdom of the Bible to help you better understand the broken pieces of your life. We are on a journey to discover that the cracks in our lives are not flaws - they are making us whole. Here is what to expect each day:

SHE EMBRACES THE CRACKS: Each day will open with a section called, "Embracing the Cracks." You will find a Bible Verse, Truth Statement®, and introduction to that day's topic with some personal reflection from Raychel. This section will help you frame your mind and prepare you for the content for that day.

SHE IS DETERMINED: This section will help you dig deep into the Word of God on that day's topic. You will find space to write as you answer questions and explore what God has to say about embracing your broken pieces.

SHE IS UNBROKEN: This is your journal and reflection space to help you apply what you are learning. This final section of your daily devotional is filled with thought provoking and strategic questions.

HOW TO USE YOUR TRUTH STATEMENT®: A Truth Statement® is a coaching concept we developed at RAYMA Team, LLC to help build your faith, overcome fear and doubt, and boost your confidence. It is really the art of personalizing God's Word and speaking to it over your life. It helps remind you of who you want to be, and rewires your brain with truth.

Say your Truth Statement® out loud every day. Yes, out loud. And yes, it feels weird if you have never done this before. Do it anyway. Ready? Let's get started...

INTRO:

IT STARTS WITH A CHOICE

Mom! It's a picture of a life moment!" With those words my precious, bubbly, blonde three-year-old handed me a piece of folded up cardboard like it was the greatest treasure on earth. "Don't drop it," she said as she bounded away to play in the grass with her siblings.

As I sat there holding that scrap of paper in my hand, I grabbed my phone and took a quick selfie. I needed to document this "life moment." As I looked at the photo, I teared up when I realized I saw something in my eyes I hadn't seen in a long time. I saw determination and strength.

The truth is, a few days before, I had a choice to make. I found myself walking through a familiar storm that was threatening to tear apart my family and leave me with nothing but broken pieces and shattered dreams. At first, I was angry that God was making us walk through this storm again. Didn't we learn the lesson last time? I had a choice to make. I could stay angry, or I could choose to walk forward with faith.

I chose to walk forward. I chose to no longer be a victim to the circumstances in my life - or the storm I found myself in. I chose to rise up and fight. I may be taking one day at a time. I may be sad and a little disappointed that I'm walking through a season I thought I would never have to walk through again. But I am not a victim.

Neither are you. It's time to make a choice. It's time to embrace the beauty of your brokenness. It's time to rise up in faith and walk boldly into the storm knowing God's got your back. It's time to find your story in the wounds and scars. It's time to overcome the sadness, the bitterness, the un-forgiveness, the worry, and the doubt.

Girl! It's time to grab hold of the promises of God and find your tenacity and strength. The broken pieces of your life are creating a beautiful masterpiece. Find your courage dear one! It's the cracks that are making you whole.

Much Love,
~Raychel

DAY 1:
YOUR FIRST CHOICE

"I have told you these things, so that in me you may have peace. In this world you will have trouble. But take heart! I have overcome the world."
~John 16:33

TRUTH STATEMENT®

When bad things happen to me,
I will choose faith, forgiveness,
restoration, hope, and healing.

SHE EMBRACES THE CRACKS...

We use many words to describe the painful experiences in our lives. Maybe you call them troubles, tests, trials, afflictions, or even seasons. I like to use the word "storms." Storms come in with little or no warning, can cause brokenness and devastation, and will change everything in mere seconds.

Life isn't fair. I have experienced the type of storms where you can only ask, "Why?" as you look around what was once your happy life in disbelief. I have walked through the kind of pain where your entire world is changed in an instant. I have survived the storms that force us to face the frailty of humanity and the cruel reality of a sinful world. I have been broken.

Jesus tells us there will be trouble in this world. We really shouldn't be shocked by it, but we are! How often have you been sucker punched by a storm where the severity, length, and even the outcome leaves you disoriented and searching for answers? You might be walking through a storm like that right now. If you are, you are in good company.

I have been completely shocked by the storms that have come through my life. I certainly didn't see them coming! Those storms came into my life with no warning at all.

There was no warning when my parents divorced when I was 15. There were few hints that my marriage would go through seasons so violent they would shake me to my very core. I didn't get a heads up when a trusted mentor betrayed me. There was no notification that depression and anxiety would be nearly constant companions in my adult life, or that the darkest seasons would happen while bringing three beautiful babies into the world.

You don't get to choose what kinds of storms you will survive. Or the level of brokenness, pain, and scars you will experience. The storms will rarely come with a warning. The first choice you get to make is how you will respond.

You can choose faith or you can choose doubt.

You can choose to be an overcomer or you can choose to stay a victim.

You can choose hope or you can choose fear.

You choose healing or you can choose to stay broken.

You can choose to restore & forgive or you can choose bitterness.

The choice, dear friend, is all up to you.

SHE IS DETERMINED...

> *"I have told you these things, so that in me you may have peace. In this world you will have trouble. But take heart! I have overcome the world." ~John 16:33*

In the NIV version of John 16:33, the author uses the word "trouble" to describe the grief Jesus' disciples are about to experience leading up to the crucifixion. I would hardly use the word "trouble" to describe something like that! Sometimes our English words fail at expressing the real meanings so let's look at this word in its original Greek context.

> ***Thlipsis:*** *Greek. Noun. Trouble, distress, oppression, or tribulation. (Edward W. Goodrick, 2004)*

Doesn't that describe the storms in your life a little better? It does for me! The Bible uses the word *thlipsis* in seven different verses in the New Testament. Look up each one of these verses below and record what you learn as you dig deeper into the meaning of the word "trouble" and how you should respond to it.

> *Tip: Make sure you read the verses before and after each highlighted section-so you can understand the context.*

- Matthew 13:21 & Mark 4:17 (The Parable of the Sower)

- Romans 2:9

- Romans 8:35

- 2 Corinthians 1:4

- Philippians 1:17

- 2 Thessalonians 1:6

SHE IS UNBROKEN...

In the past, how did you respond to the storms, and cracks, in your life?

In the future, how could you respond to a storm in your life that better lines up with God's truth?

What is God saying to you as you complete today's study?

DAY 2:

CHOOSING TRUTH

"When I consider your heavens, the work of your fingers, the moon and the stars, which you have set in place, what is mankind that you are mindful of them, human beings that you care for them? You have made them a little lower than the angels and crowned them with glory and honor." ~Psalm 8:3-5

TRUTH STATEMENT®

I am created in God's image. When lies and labels threaten to steal my identity, I will remind myself that I am God's masterpiece.

SHE EMBRACES THE CRACKS...

"What if they were right? What if I really am a crappy writer and I don't have any discernment or wisdom? Because if they were right, I am clearly completely unqualified to write this Bible study."

As soon as the words came out of my mouth, I knew they were lies. They were labels I had been carrying around for years. Even though all evidence pointed to the contrary. My head knew. But my heart was still struggling to erase the memories of what was said.

My husband looked at me like I had three heads and said, "Who said that to you?" I replied, "You know." Wanting to avoid the question he would ask me next. "Say it out loud. Who said that to you?" I started to cry as I listed the names of the leaders who had spoken death over me and my gifts. I knew that once the lies were out of my head, I could defeat them with truth.

Those lies came from some of the cruelest storms of my life. Storms that made me question who I was and what I was called to do. Storms that created cracks so deep I gave up on my God-given calling for a season because of fear and doubt.

God takes shame and self-image very seriously, especially the lies and the labels. He created you in His image and you reflect His character and His attributes.

> *"So God created mankind in his own image, in the image of God he created them. Male and female he created them." ~Genesis 1:27*

No one else has the power to change the masterpiece He created you to be. But, if we are being honest with each other, how often do we struggle with what someone has said about us - even decades later? How many life-altering storms have changed our perception of truth and covered us with lies? We can be full of cracks that gnaw away at our rightful calling and destiny. How many labels define us even though we know deep down they are not true? I bet you have more lies and labels than you probably care to think about. We all do.

Who told you that you were broken? That you were damaged, incapable, not smart enough, unworthy, or that you can't? Shame is an incredibly powerful tool Satan uses to keep us in an endless cycle of doubt and ineffectiveness. He has been using this tactic since the Garden of Eden. It's time for the cycle to stop. Let's embrace the truth of who God says we are.

SHE IS DETERMINED...

Let's dig a little deeper into how God views shame, lies, and labels. First, look up Genesis Chapters 2 & 3 in your favorite version of the Bible and read it. You will notice that the word "Naked" is used four different times. You can find the verses on the next page:

"And they were both naked, the man and his wife, and were not ashamed." ~Genesis 2:25 (NKJV)

"Then the eyes of both of them were opened, and they knew that they were naked; and they sewed fig leaves together and made themselves coverings." ~Genesis 3:7 (NKJV)

"So he said, "I heard your voice in the garden, and I was afraid because I was naked; and I hid myself." ~Genesis 3:10 (NKJV)

"And he said, "Who told you that you were naked? Have you eaten from the tree of which I commanded you that you should not eat?" ~Genesis 3:11 (NKJV)

They all sound about the same don't they? But, if you look at the Hebrew words that are used in the original context, you will notice a big difference between the meanings. In Genesis 2:25 the Hebrew word *ārum* is used. This word is an adjective, which means naked or stripped. In Genesis 3:7, 10, and 11 the Hebrew word is *erōm*. This word is used as a noun, which means naked, or nakedness. (Edward W. Goodrick, 2004)

In case it's been awhile since you were in English class, a noun is a person, place, or thing and an adjective is a word or phrase that describes or modifies a noun. That means when Genesis 2:25 describes Adam and Eve as naked it is just describing an attribute of them. They were naked. You could also say their hair is brown. But, *after* they eat from the tree, and shame enters in, the word naked switches to a noun. All of a sudden what was supposed to be a part of their identity becomes their entire identity.

Let that sink in for a minute.

The good news is God could not leave them with an identity of sin and shame. So, He put in motion a plan to send His Son to the world to save them from this identity crisis. How amazing is that! The lies and labels that swirl around in your head are not your identity. Even if you did something that justifies you carrying one label or another. Your past is a part of your story - not your entire story. Dear friend, He wants us to be set free from this shame.

Your scars and cracks are your testimony. You are not broken. You are His masterpiece.

SHE IS UNBROKEN...

Record below the lies and labels you struggle with and who spoke them over you. (Don't forget the lies and labels you've spoken over yourself!)

Take a few moments and think about what you learned while studying the word "naked" in Genesis 2 & 3. How does this make you feel about your own struggles with labels and feeling broken?

What is God saying to you as you complete today's study?

DAY 3:

CHOOSING GRATITUDE

"Do not be anxious about anything, but in every situation, by prayer and petition, with thanksgiving, present your requests to God." ~Philippians 4:6

TRUTH STATEMENT®

I choose to be grateful in all circumstances.

SHE EMBRACES THE CRACKS...

I love the iconic John Hughes movies of the 1980's. Movies like *Pretty in Pink*, *The Breakfast Club*, *Sixteen Candles*, and so many more defined a generation as teenage angst spread across the silver screen. We watched the geek end up with the prom queen, the lonely neglected girl find her prince, the rebel reformed by love, and life end happily ever after in 90 short minutes. It is glorious. It is an entertaining escape from reality. But it isn't real.

John Hughes does not direct my life. That means that resolutions may not come quickly. Love might not conquer all this side of Heaven. Loneliness will happen more than I want. Dreams won't always come true. People will hurt and betray me.

Let's face it the road to "happily ever after" is nothing like those iconic movies. Maybe that's why I love them so much. When life gets too hard and too overwhelming a 90-minute break in a world where everything turns out right is sometimes just what my weary heart needs.

I can almost guarantee you have wanted to scream, "Life sucks!" and throw yourself one heck of a pity party a time or two. I get it. There have been times in my life when the marriage was too hard, the mental illness too strong, and the future too bleak that I've wanted to give up in despair. Oh my goodness, self-pity was once my best friend and making the people around me suffer for my unfair life was the mission.

> ***Self-pity:*** *Noun. A feeling of pity for yourself because you believe you have suffered more than is fair or reasonable. (Merriam-Webster.com, 2011)*

Self-pity is a tricky little poison that will eventually destroy you. It starts out innocent enough, with a storm. One terrible storm that completely shakes you to your core and changes your environment, and your future, in minutes. When storms like that happen you have the right to be angry and sad and hurt and you need to express those feelings. But, if you are not careful, those feelings can keep you in a cycle of bitterness and un-forgiveness for years. Especially if those feelings pile up from storms you've never gotten over.

Self-pity is a time robber and life stealer. It keeps us screaming and yelling about the broken pieces in our lives and demanding revenge. We are so distracted with proving to everyone how unfair our life is, we forget to find some glue and put it all back together. We must feel the deep pain of the storms that rage in our lives; but we must also learn when it's time to stop feeling sorry for ourselves, pick up our mats, and walk.

SHE IS DETERMINED...

How do you feel deep pain and sorrow and not spiral into self-pity forever? By choosing gratitude. Gratitude stops self-pity in its tracks! It is scientifically proven that gratitude improves your life physically, mentally, emotionally, and relationally. Gratitude is a spiritual discipline that will help you defeat self-pity even in the midst of horrible circumstances. However, it does not come naturally. It is a weapon that you need to continually sharpen. Gratitude takes your eyes off of the storm raging around you and puts them on the One who controls the wind and the waves.

"It is good to give thanks to the LORD, to sing praises to the Most High." ~Psalm 92:1 (NLT)

Take some time to look up these verses about gratitude in the midst of trials. Jot down a few notes as you read them. Focus on how gratitude can help you defeat self-pity and have the right perspective when you are experiencing storms in your life.

- Psalm 50:23

- Romans 12:12

- Philippians 4:6-7

- James 1:2

- James 1:12

SHE IS UNBROKEN...

How has self-pity caused you to lose precious time and kept you stuck in your life?

Take a few moments and think about some of the biggest storms of your life – the moments where you have felt the most broken – and start writing a gratitude list of everything good that came from those seasons in your life. Set a timer for five minutes and start writing!!

DAY 4:

CHOOSING COURAGE

"I will not be afraid because the Lord is with me." ~Psalm 118:6 (EXB)

TRUTH STATEMENT®

I can trust God in the midst of uncertainty. I will not live my life in fear.

SHE EMBRACES THE CRACKS...

"Love is what you were born with, fear is what you learned." ~Unknown

I don't know when the love you were born with was replaced by fear. Maybe your innocence was taken at a very young age. Or you learned the harsh reality of life and death before you were old enough to understand what you were going through. Or, maybe you grew up in a violent home and experienced trauma as a child. It's possible the circumstances of your life taught you to feed your fear instead of defeat it.

For much of my life I wore the label *fear* like it was my identity. I made the choice to grow bitter and fearful because of the storms I had walked through. The broken pieces of my life made me full of fear. I was terrified of the unknown and eventually this led to things like: mediocrity, unfulfilled dreams, toxic relationships, missed opportunities, anxiety, panic attacks, shallow faith, depression, paralyzing doubt, feeling stuck, being unable to make decisions, and excuses. Oh the excuses.

Over the last few years I have found that the best way to defeat fear is with action. We can take action in the midst of being afraid. Because, the truth is, fear is not the same thing as being afraid. Fear will make us self-sabotage relationships when vulnerability is required for growth. It makes us say or think things like, "I can't," "I don't know how," or "It's never going to work out." Fear keeps us stuck in excuses for years. Which then makes us spin our wheels and miss out on once-in-a-life-time opportunities.

Walking forward even though we are afraid is motivating. Doing something afraid can propel us into new seasons and healing we never imagined possible.

> ***Courage:*** *Noun. Mental or moral strength to venture, persevere, and withstand danger, fear, or difficulty. (Merriam-Webster.com, 2011)*

It takes great courage to take a step of faith when you have no idea where your foot may land. A person who embraces the cracks in her life defeats fear and walks forward… even when she is afraid. As you continue with today's study you will learn the difference between the words "fear" and "afraid." You will examine the different ways these words are used in the Bible and how understanding the meanings can help you better overcome the storms. By the end of this study, you will be ready to muster up your courage and walk forward – especially when you are afraid.

SHE IS DETERMINED…

> ***Fear:*** *Noun. A distressing emotion aroused by impending danger, evil, pain, etc., whether the threat is real or imagined; the feeling or condition of being afraid. Synonyms: foreboding, apprehension, consternation, dismay, dread, terror, fright, panic, horror, trepidation. (Merriam-Webster.com, 2011)*

> ***Afraid:*** *Adjective. Feeling fear; filled with apprehension: afraid to go. Feeling regret, unhappiness, or the like. Feeling reluctance, unwillingness, distaste. Synonyms: scared, fearful, disquieted, apprehensive, timid, timorous. (Merriam-Webster.com, 2011)*

In many English versions of the Bible, the words *fear* and *afraid* are often used interchangeably. But they shouldn't be. For example, a commonly used Hebrew word for fear in the Old Testament is *yārā* which has a few different meanings. Sometimes it means the kind of fear that is akin to honor, respect, and awe (ie: "the fear of the Lord.") Other times it means to frighten, terrify or intimidate. Those are two very different meanings of the word *fear* that should create two very different responses in the believer's life.

Look up these following verses. Record the differences you notice in how the word *fear* is used. What do you discover about fear as it relates to the storms, and the broken pieces in your life?

- Joshua 24:14
- Psalm 56:3
- Psalm 112:7
- John 14:27
- Romans 8:15

SHE IS UNBROKEN...

In your own words, what is the difference between the words *fear* and *afraid*?

How can this difference help you better handle the broken pieces of your life and get a better perspective of your future?

What worries you about releasing fear and embracing trust, patience, or forgiveness?

DAY 5:

CHOOSING TRUST

"Trust in the Lord with all your heart and lean not on your own understanding." ~Proverbs 3:5

TRUTH STATEMENT®

My God is faithful and trustworthy. I have no reason to doubt or fear.

SHE EMBRACES THE CRACKS...

Our marriage was in trouble for many years. We were a ticking time bomb and it was only going to be a matter of time before I made good on my back up plan and walked out the door for good. I believed I tried everything in my power to fix our marriage. I prayed. I read books. I consulted others. I ignored the problems and hoped they would go away. I raged and gave ultimatums.

One day at a prayer service, during a real hard season where I contemplated leaving for the second time, I heard God say in an audible voice like He was sitting right next to me. *"Why do you keep standing in the way of what I want to do? When are you going to get out of the way?"* I was shocked by the directness. I was not sure how to respond. All I could think was, *"Because I'm scared."* God said to me, *"I know. But I promise to take care of you and your child if you will just get out of the way."*

Over the next eight years, God worked on my heart. It took much longer than I expected for that tiny seed of faith to start bearing fruit. When I would doubt God, and try and take back control, I would find myself with wounds I was never intended to bear. Learning that God was trustworthy no matter what storms were raging in my life, or what other people did, was a major battle I fought for years.

Choosing to trust God with my life and my future was the most important choice I ever made. That choice was the first step in my journey to embracing the cracks that were making me whole. Take my hand dear lady and let's walk forward together.

SHE IS DETERMINED...

Look up Psalm 22 in your favorite version of the Bible and read it all the way through. Now, let's dig deeper into King David's model for defeating fear and doubt and building trust in the God who has proven himself trustworthy.

Step #1: Acknowledge (Psalm 22:1-2)

You need to acknowledge the doubt and the fear that God can't hear you, is ignoring you, or doesn't care about you, just like King David did. Refusing to acknowledge anger, sadness, fear, and doubt is dangerous and you will become a ticking time bomb.

Step #2: Remind (Psalm 22:3-5)

Remind yourself of the things He has done for you, for your family, and even your spiritual ancestors in the Bible. Remind yourself of how God has proven himself faithful to you in your past.

Step #3: Ignore (Psalm 22:6-8)

If King David had people mocking him and thinking he was crazy when he trusted God in the midst of hopeless circumstances, you will too. It's been said that Christians are the only people who kick their own wounded. So don't be surprised when you have haters and naysayers. Ignore and forgive.

Step #4: Remember (Psalm 22:9-10)

You have to continually remember the times when God was there for you in the past to defeat the doubt and fear that pops up while you are walking through a storm. It's so important to remind yourself of God's faithfulness and truth that King David includes it twice!

Step #5: Tell (Psalm 22:11-21)

Tell God your troubles. Tell Him of the reality or your situation. Remind Him of His promises. And ask Him to intervene on your behalf.

Step #6: Praise & Declare (Psalm 22:22-31)

Praise God in the midst of trial because it will calm your spirit and help you focus on the good and not the bad all the time. Praise develops a heart of gratitude. Praise is a small escape from your current reality where you can declare truth and remind yourself of God's faithfulness and promised victory.

SHE IS UNBROKEN...

Ask God to reveal any emotions (anger, fear, doubt, or sadness, etc.) that need to be brought to light so they can be healed. Write down what He is telling you:

How has God proven Himself faithful to you in your past?

What is God saying to you as you complete today's study?

DAY 6:

CHOOSING CERTAINTY

"May the God of hope fill you with all joy and peace in believing, so that by the power of the Holy Spirit you may abound in hope." ~Romans 15:13 ESV

TRUTH STATEMENT®

When worries bombard me, I will remind myself that I can trust in the certainty of my God. I choose hope. I have no reason to worry because He will not fail me.

SHE EMBRACES THE CRACKS…

> ***Worry*** **-** *Verb. To torment oneself with or suffer from disturbing thoughts. (Merriam-Webster.com, 2011)*

Yeesh. Torment isn't a word I would toss around lightly, would you? Yet, so often we act like worrying is no big deal. We worry, we fret, and we obsess about everything. We even get together with our friends to hash over everything that has worried us. It's almost like worry is just an accepted part of being human. Why is that?

When I read the definition of worry, all I can think is that worrying is quite literally emotional and mental torture and is very much a BIG deal. For many seasons of my life, I was plagued by worry. And I'm not talking about the everyday worries we brush by as normal. I was emotionally and mentally tortured by something called Postpartum Obsessive Compulsive Disorder (PPOCD) after every one of my pregnancies.

If you are not familiar with perinatal mood disorders you might not realize there was any other diagnosis for a woman to receive after giving birth than Postpartum Depression, but there are many. One of the key symptoms of Postpartum OCD is intrusive thoughts. (Postpartum Progress, n.d.) The best way to describe intrusive thoughts is to take the normal nagging fears of your child being hurt and twist them until they are ugly, horrific nightmares that plague you constantly.

You can't shake it. You can't reason with it. You can't stop it. You can't tell anyone what is happening because who says out loud "Every time I'm at the top of a staircase I imagine throwing the baby down." Um. No one. I was trapped in my own brain with a personal invitation to a private hell only I knew was happening. I'm not exaggerating when I say my worst season of my PPOCD lasted almost 18 months and those kinds of thoughts would happen hourly.

It is so traumatic, that women who suffer from PPOCD are often diagnosed with PTSD afterwards. (Postpartum Progress, n.d.)

I am the first to admit the cracks from those seasons of my life are deep and just barely healed in some places - and that the thoughts still return even years later. The only way I overcome the worry is by reminding myself of the truth that no matter what happens to my children, even if every horrific thing my mind thought up occurred, God is still in control. He would make them whole again and turn their brokenness into beauty just like he did for me. Admitting the brokenness I experienced because of those seasons, and still choosing to rest in the certainty of my God, is how I'm embracing those scars.

SHE IS DETERMINED...

Even if you have never experienced the kind of thoughts I have, I know you can understand and relate to worry being the thoughts that literally torment you. We all have worry and we need to combat it instead of letting it go like it's normal or to be expected. Worry is not from God. Worry is like fear and needs to be confronted right away before it consumes you and poisons you from the inside out.

Let's dig into the Word to see what God says about how we can (and must!) choose certainty in the midst of our worries and fears*. After you read the verses below, take a few moments to record how these promises can help you defeat worry and choose certainty instead:

"Even though I walk through the darkest valley, I will fear no evil, for you are with me; your rod and your staff, they comfort me." ~Psalm 23:4

"Peace I leave with you; my peace I give you. I do not give to you as the world gives. Do not let your hearts be troubled and do not be afraid." ~John 14:27

"Humble yourselves, therefore, under God's mighty hand, that he may lift you up in due time. Cast all your anxiety on him because he cares for you." ~I Peter 5:6-8

"But now thus says the LORD, he who created you, O Jacob, he who formed you, O Israel: "Fear not, for I have redeemed you; I have called you by name, you are mine. When you pass through the waters, I will

be with you; and through the rivers, they shall not overwhelm you; when you walk through fire you shall not be burned, and the flame shall not consume you. For I am the LORD your God, the Holy One of Israel, your Savior." ~Isaiah 43:1-3

*To the beautiful mommy reading this thinking, "Oh my gosh I think that's what I have!" Please hear me when I say that PPOCD is a mood disorder and will usually require medication and therapy to overcome. While these Bible verses will bring you comfort, they should not replace proper treatment. There is ZERO shame in getting all the help you need to overcome this.

SHE IS UNBROKEN...

Does the dictionary definition of worry make you think any differently about the effect it has in your life? Why or why not?

How can you choose certainty over worry? Write down some specific action steps you can take when worry starts to overwhelm you:

What is God saying to you as you complete today's study?

DAY 7:

CHOOSING TO OVERCOME

"But we do not belong to those who shrink back and are destroyed, but to those who have faith and are saved." ~Hebrews 10:39

TRUTH STATEMENT®

I am patient and will persevere. I will endure because I am an overcomer.

SHE EMBRACES THE CRACKS...

What is it that makes one person rise up in the midst of horrific circumstances and overcome and another succumb to the despair and remain a victim? Victor Frankl, a Jewish Austrian neurologist and psychiatrist, developed an existential theory called logotherapy. Logotherapy is based on the premise that if people could find meaning in their lives, they could endure even the most brutal hardship. If they could find a *WHY* they could endure almost any *HOW*. Before he founded this theory, Victor Frankl spent three years in Nazi concentration camps.

In 1937, after great success in treating patients with depression and suicidal tendencies during his residency, Frankl started his own private practice in Vienna, Austria. One year later, Austria was invaded by Nazi Germany and Frankl was forced to work only with Jewish patients. In 1940, Frankl started working at Rothschild Hospital and because of his medical expertise managed to save several patients from the Nazi Euthanasia program. In September of 1942 Frankl, his wife Tilly, and his mother and father were all sent to the Theresienstadt Ghetto.

Theresienstadt was part ghetto part concentration camp that served as a holding cell until prisoners were sent to other camps. While there, Frankl's skills were recognized and he was allowed to work with incoming prisoners to help them overcome shock and grief. His father died at Theresienstadt. In October of 1944, Frankl and his wife Tilly were transferred to Auschwitz, where they were processed and sent to Kaufering and Bergen-Belson respectively. Frankl worked for five months as a slave laborer at Kaufering before he was transferred again to Turkheim. He worked as a physician at Turkheim until he was liberated by US soldiers in 1945.

Frankl's mother and brother would die at Auschwitz and Tilly at Bergen-Belson. Frankl and his sister were the only survivors. What he discovered about human behavior during the three years in those concentration camps shaped his entire life's work. He observed by living and working with his fellow prisoners that if people could find meaning and a why, they could endure even the most horrific circumstances. He discovered that hope, and a reason to keep living, helped them endure circumstances so horrible many gave up in despair and died. (Wikipedia, n.d.)

What about you? Do you have a *why* that helps you endure any storm in your life? Do you believe there is a greater purpose for your broken pieces? Do you have what it takes to rise above the horrible pain in your past? I believe you do, dear friend, and it's time to remind yourself that you were born an overcomer.

SHE IS DETERMINED...

> *"If we have our own why in life, we shall get along with almost any how."*
> *~Friedrich Nietzsche* (Nietzsche, 1997)

> ***Perseverance:*** *Noun. The quality that allows someone to continue trying to do something even though it is difficult. Synonyms: tenacity, endurance, steadfastness. (Merriam-Webster.com, 2011)*

hupomoné: *Greek. Noun, Feminine. A remaining behind, a patient enduring. (Edward W. Goodrick, 2004)*

When I think of stories like Victor Frankl's, and others who survive horrific circumstances in their lives, I admire their courage and their perseverance. It's because they found a reason to endure their suffering that they came out of the storm as overcomers, not as victims. That is the kind of person I want to be!

Today, spend some time looking up the following verses on perseverance and see what God says about the meaning of trials and discovering your "why." Jot down any personal reflections after each verse.

- Luke 21:19

- Romans 5:3-5

- Romans 8:25-28

- I Corinthians 1:6-9

- Hebrews 10:36-39

- 2 Peter 1:5-8

SHE IS UNBROKEN…

What are a few of the benefits you discovered from today's study about choosing to overcome and persevere instead of giving up? Write them below:

Write down the Bible verse/s that meant the most to you from the previous section:

What is God saying to you as you complete today's study?

DAY 8:

ACCEPTING REALITY

"I have told you this so that through me you may have peace. In the world you'll have trouble but be courageous - I've overcome the world!" ~John 16:33

TRUTH STATEMENT®

When I accept the reality of the storms in my life, and the broken pieces they create, I can accept the healing I need to move forward.

SHE EMBRACES THE CRACKS...

Have you ever walked through a storm in your life and you were the last to know? I have. You are probably thinking, "Raychel, how could you not know you were in the middle of a storm?" The storm was raging inside my own head and I did not even know it was there. I accepted the labels of *crazy* and *angry* for so long I could no longer see the truth from the lie. I was so completely clueless to my own battle in the middle of one of the worst seasons with depression, I told my two best friends, "It's a good thing my life is under control, because you guys are falling apart!" They don't let me live that down. It's OK. it keeps me humble. *wink*

What is it about storms in your life that makes you think that if you ignore them they will go away? In my experience, this has worked zero times. None. Nada. On Day 6, I shared with you what it was like having PPOCD and being plagued by constant worry. Today I want to tell you about how I finally accepted the reality that I was actually in the middle of a storm. I was so used to wearing the labels I couldn't see the truth that I wasn't crazy… I was sick. Ignoring my depression, and believing that I really was a sad angry crazy person, was only making it worse and prolonging my healing.

A few weeks after our youngest was born I was hosting a party. At some point in the evening, I started sharing about this "event" (i.e. - panic attack) that had happened with me, and my husband, a few nights earlier. As I told the women this story, I could literally see the expression on their faces change. It went from calm to horror in about three seconds flat. My mom reached over and grabbed my hand and said, "Honey, do you think you might be experiencing some postpartum depression?"

Later that night I started Googling my symptoms (because that's the sane thing to do when you think something is wrong with you) and found Postpartum Progress. I read the stories of the Warrior Moms and cried all night. I realized I wasn't crazy. I wasn't broken beyond repair. I wasn't alone. You see, I was believing a lie. A lie is a lie even if you chose to believe it. That night changed everything.

I finally found the answer! That night helped me accept the reality of the storm I was walking through. And, because I accepted the reality, I could now accept help and healing. Dear brave woman of God, you can't heal what you don't acknowledge. Let's find healing together.

SHE IS DETERMINED...

When you cannot accept the reality of your situation, you prolong the pain and the brokenness because you cannot take steps towards healing. Today, let's explore different verses that will help you better understand the beauty of accepting a harsh reality and moving forward. These verses are beautiful promises of God meant to give you peace in the midst of uncertainty. As you look up each verse, or verses, take some time and jot down what it means to you:

- Romans 8:37-39

- Romans 10:9-10

- Galatians 5:1

- Philippians 4:13-15

- 2 Timothy 4:17

SHE IS UNBROKEN...

What does refusing to accept the reality of a storm in your life cost you?

How does accepting the reality of the broken pieces in your life benefit you?

Write down the Bible verses that meant the most to you from the previous section:

DAY 9:
ACCEPTING GOD'S TIMING

"To everything there is a season, and a time for every purpose under heaven."
~Ecclesiastes 3:1

TRUTH STATEMENT®

God's timing is perfect even when I do not understand it.

SHE EMBRACES THE CRACKS...

We have a running joke in the office that we are always off on the timing of launching an event, coaching program, or product. Always. It has happened so often that we now call it a blessing because it's forced us to jump in and try something - even if we don't know the outcome. If I've learned anything while on this journey to embrace the cracks that are making me whole, it's that God's timing is rarely the same as mine.

When it comes to the who, what, when, where, and why of the storms in our lives we will always be off on the timing. Because, let's face it, if it was up to us we would just skip the storms all together. We would leap over the pain. We would avoid the changes they bring. We would skip the inconvenience, anger, disappointment, and the unanswered questions. And, most especially, the breaking.

Wouldn't it be wonderful if we could learn perseverance without having to actually persevere through something? But that is not how God teaches His children to trust Him. One of the ways we learn to trust Him is by learning to accept HIS timing. You can have all your ducks in a row but if your timing does not match His it won't matter what you do, those ducks will all wander off!

I've learned it's best to trust God has a plan. I trust His timing is better than mine even when I can't understand it. I am learning to wait. No, I don't like it. No, I'm not always great at it. But, whenever I've been impatient in the past and tried to control the outcome, minimize the risk, or simply go chasing after those dumb ducks, I've made a messy situation even worse.

Learning to accept God's timing and wait is a spiritual discipline we all should develop. We waste so much time lamenting the storms in our lives that we miss the blessings found in the brokenness. We cry so long over all the broken pieces that we miss the message in all the mess. Learning to listen for that still small voice in the midst of the chaos is how to stop jumping ahead of God's timing. He promises to give you wisdom if you will only ask. But you have to quit complaining long enough to hear His answer.

When I run ahead of God and try to make things happen in my own time, I often miss what I'm supposed to be learning during the storm.

He does not promise us a time frame. He doesn't promise that we will fully understand every storm that comes our way, or even a resolution we will like this side of Heaven. But He does promise to speak in the midst of the messiness and give us the next step if we will only listen. Isn't it time we stop and listen?

SHE IS DETERMINED...

How many times have you looked back on your life with regret because you didn't wait for God's timing? Or, how often have you looked back on your life with relief because you did wait for God's timing? Maybe you discovered that the thing you wanted so desperately was actually completely wrong for you. Can you look back on your life and see how you were saved from a painful lesson simply because you trusted God's timing?

Today we are going to explore the story of Rebecca in the book of Genesis. Rebecca was a woman who at the end of her life, like many of us, could look back and see both the blessings of accepting God's timing and the folly of rushing ahead of Him.

Read Genesis 24:1-58 and then list all the blessings Rebecca received because she was willing to accept God's timing. *(No this is not a typo. Yes, I realize how many verses that is. Now go read *wink*)*

Read Genesis 27:1-17, 41-46 and then list all off the suffering Rebecca, and her family, endured because she rushed ahead of God's timing.

SHE IS UNBROKEN...

As you look back on your own life, what are the blessings you have received because you waited on God's timing? List them below:

What are some of the consequences you, or your family, have experienced because you were impatient and jumped ahead of God's timing?

What is God saying to you as you complete today's study?

DAY 10:

ACCEPTING DISAPPOINTMENT

"Do not be quickly provoked in your spirit, for anger resides in the lap of fools."
~Ecclesiastes 7:9

TRUTH STATEMENT®

God promises me the blessings of obedience when I choose to embrace my suffering instead of anger and bitterness.

SHE EMBRACES THE CRACKS...

Have you ever gotten angry at God because you were so surprised and disappointed in how something turned out? Especially when He asks you to do something in obedience and the outcome was not at all what you were expecting? During one of those times in my life I wrote this in my journal during a time of prayer:

> *"What was the point of that? Did I just destroy people I love by telling the truth? Am I really that horribly selfish? What is the matter with me? Really, God?!"*

I was angry. Really angry. I felt like God had set me up. I was practically yelling at Him because I couldn't see the "why" to the messy situation I found myself in. I thought obedience would bring healing and restoration, not more pain and confusion. I was sad. I was shocked. I was embarrassed. I was mad.

I was walking through the restoration process with a friend, and at that time all I could feel was disappointed for how things were progressing. I was angry and unhappy. But I ultimately had a choice. I could dig my heels in and refuse to accept the emotional demands of restoration and forgiveness. I could demand my way and hurt other people. I would force an ending I thought was more appropriate. However, I knew my disobedience would come at a price.

So, I made the choice to walk through the disappointment and the anger. I chose to walk through the restoration process; and, I was rewarded with seeing a friendship restored. I chose to not rush the process or force my own agenda. I chose to implement new behaviors. I chose to forgive myself and others and start fresh. It's one of those times I will be able to look back on with gratitude because I didn't rush the process or jump ahead of God's timing. I chose to obey and embrace the suffering.

Obedience is often painful *and* beautiful. Mending the deep cracks in our lives requires sacrifice. When storms come into your life and bring with it the cracks of anger and disappointment, you will feel like you are walking through the most painful of endings. You will be mad, sad, and confused. You think, "Why me?"

Can I just remind you that there is beauty in endings if you are willing to look for it? The road will not be easy, but I can promise you that our God is faithful. I chose to walk through a painful ending with bravery, obedience, and the promise of a new beginning. What will you choose?

SHE IS DETERMINED...

Obedient *Noun. Willing to obey. Synonyms: compliant, docile, tractable, yielding, deferential, respectful. (Merriam-Webster.com, 2011)*

"Then he went down to Nazareth with them and was obedient to them. But his mother treasured all these things in her heart." ~Luke 2:51

"Who, being in very nature God, did not consider equality with God something to be used to his own advantage; rather, he made himself nothing by taking the very nature of a servant, being made in human

likeness. And being found in appearance as a man, he humbled himself by becoming obedient to death—even death on a cross!" ~Philippians 2:6-8

"During the days of Jesus' life on earth, he offered up prayers and petitions with fervent cries and tears to the one who could save him from death, and he was heard because of his reverent submission. Son though he was, he learned obedience from what he suffered." ~Hebrews 5:7-8

I was surprised to discover how many times the words obedient and obedience described Jesus in the Bible. From the time He was a child until He was an adult His life was marked by obedience. You might be thinking, "Well of course He was obedient, He was Jesus." Not exactly. Hebrews 5:8 tells us He *learned* obedience. He wasn't born into this world knowing how to obey.

Jesus put aside His sovereignty and embraced His humanity so He could gain the blessings of obedience through suffering. We learn how to obey just like Jesus did by being willing to suffer and be broken. We learn obedience through brokenness! There are beautiful blessings in obedience described in the Bible. A few of the blessings include prosperity, a long life that bears good fruit, and being loved by God.

Look up Deuteronomy Chapter 28 and read what is described as "Blessings for Obedience." Write below the many blessings that are listed:

SHE IS UNBROKEN...

Describe a time when God's answer was "No" and how you reacted to that situation:

How does it make you feel that Jesus had to learn to be obedient by being willing to suffer?

What is God saying to you as you complete today's study?

DAY 11:
ACCEPTING FORGIVENESS

"I tell you, her sins - and they are many - have been forgiven, so she has shown me much love. But a person who is forgiven little shows only little love."
~Luke 7:47

TRUTH STATEMENT®

I am forgiven. I am free. I am whole.

SHE EMBRACES THE CRACKS...

I used to believe that as long as I refused to forgive, I had the power. That somehow I was powerful enough to protect myself from being hurt again. That me not forgiving someone who hurt me was the ultimate revenge. I believed that by a sheer act of will I could pretend I wasn't hurt and that their behavior, words, and choices didn't affect me. I had the power. I had the power. I had the power.

But, I didn't have power - I was a prisoner. I was broken. All I had was a broken heart that I was trying desperately to protect. What I had was guilt and shame. With a great deal of bitterness, sarcasm, and a critical spirit on the side. I had a thick brick wall around my heart and emotions that kept everyone out. I did not have the power at all. I was fearful, sad, and broken.

> *"Only the brave know how to forgive... a coward never forgave; it is not in his nature." ~Laurence Sterne (Sterne, 1760)*

The hardest person for me to learn to forgive was myself. It took me years to admit my own guilt when it came to some of the deepest scars in my life. Admitting that I was responsible for a lot of the chaos that whirled around in my life was a lot harder than I could have imagined. I would love to tell you that on such and such a day I decided to forgive myself and everything changed, but the truth is it wasn't that simple. Learning how to forgive myself was a daily choice and often times an uphill battle.

Here's the real kicker, until I could forgive myself for the broken pieces and the scars, I couldn't forgive anyone else either. I couldn't move forward into healing and restoration with anyone who had hurt me in the past until I could forgive myself. I had to admit my brokenness. I had to admit my guilt and shame. I had to admit my fear, bitterness, sarcasm, and critical spirit. I had to admit all of the darkness in my own heart and ask for forgiveness first. I had to find grace for myself before I could extend it to the ones who hurt me.

Maybe you know exactly what it's like to keep yourself a prisoner because of un-forgiveness. Maybe you know how it feels to be so terrified of being hurt again you turn your emotions off and you shut yourself away. It's time to be brave, dear friend, and open the door to that prison. Today is the day to choose freedom and accept forgiveness. You've waited long enough.

SHE IS DETERMINED...

> *"Bear with each other and forgive one another if any of you has a grievance against someone. Forgive as the Lord forgave you."*
> *~Colossians 3:13*

We are called to forgive one another. But did you realize that "one another" includes yourself? The word "one another" in Colossians 3:13 is the Greek word *tis,* which means one, anyone, anything, some, someone, or something. ANYONE means you. God doesn't want His precious daughters just forgiving everyone else for creating cracks and scars in their lives - He wants you to forgive yourself too. He wants to bring freedom and restoration to your life through forgiveness!

In 2013, my business partner and best-friend Mandy and I created a five-step process called "The Honor Code of Conflict Resolution." It was birthed out of one of the most painful storms and friendship conflicts we have ever had. It caused cracks so deep they took years to heal. We realized we had no idea how to forgive people who hurt us so deeply, who was not sorry, minimized the pain, and caused us to believe lies and doubt the calling God had on our lives. The Honor Code is how we were able to forgive ourselves and the people who hurt us.

The first couple steps of the honor code focus on letting time pass, acknowledging your own guilt and pain, and forgiving yourself, because conflict resolution cannot happen during high emotions. What we discovered is - you can't forgive others until you can forgive yourself. And that takes time.

> *"Repent, then, and turn to God, so that your sins may be wiped out, that times of refreshing may come from the Lord." ~Acts 3:19*

Times of refreshing. What a beautiful promise of restoration when we choose to forgive ourselves and others! Is it easy to forgive yourself? Absolutely not. Is it difficult to forgive someone who isn't sorry? Extremely. However, forgiveness is always worth it. Always.

What is God telling you as you complete today's study?

SHE IS UNBROKEN...

Spend some time in prayer and ask God to reveal any un-forgiveness in your life for yourself and for others. Then complete the following exercise:

_________________________________ (Your Name) I forgive you for:

Date: ______________________

DAY 12:

ACCEPTING PATIENCE

"A patient man has great understanding. But a quick-tempered man displays folly." ~Proverbs 14:29

TRUTH STATEMENT®

I am patient. I will wait calmly for God to bring resolution and restoration.

SHE EMBRACES THE CRACKS...

I'm not a "wait and see" kind of girl. If I see a problem, I want the solution yesterday. If I have a plan, a need, or a dream, I want to do it, fix it, and achieve it immediately. While I've come a long way with my patience, the truth is it's still a struggle sometimes. I hardly ever slow down. I demand answers and quick responses. I don't take the time to explain why very often. I rarely pause for explanations and that leads me to jump to conclusions.

I'm sometimes the worst when it comes to my kiddos. Phrases like, "Hurry up!" "Why would you do that?!" "Because I said so." "How long can it take?" come out in moments of frustration when I'm waiting on a dawdling four-year-old or at the end of my rope with an all-knowing 10-year-old. But, this is not patience. This is the exact opposite of patience. Being impatient is a horrible pattern that I have to continually work on and ask forgiveness for.

If you appreciate irony, you will love this. When I graduated high school, I won a scholarship called the "Lance and Helen Patchell Award." Know what it was for? Perseverance and patience in the midst of trials. Seriously! While I appreciate the award, that sweet 18-year-old girl knew very little about patience and perseverance.

It's true that by that time I had learned some perseverance in my life with my parent's divorce. But that young woman had only chipped the top of the iceberg for what storms she would have to walk through to teach her what patience and perseverance really meant.

She had no idea that someday she would wait years and years for God to answer her prayer and restore her heart and her marriage. She didn't have a clue what it felt like to wait months and months, and even years, for God's timing to be perfect and dreams to be realized.

For some of us, developing patience is a life-long battle. If that is you don't give up! Rise up and fight! Fight to be the kind of woman you always dreamed you would be - cracks and all. Give yourself grace when you become impatient. Ask for forgiveness when you blow it. Pick yourself up and dust yourself off and keep moving forward. Sometimes it takes time to see things clearly and understand a situation fully. Slow down, friend. Breathe. Patience is developed in the waiting.

SHE IS DETERMINED...

> ***Patient:*** *Adjective. Able to remain calm and not become annoyed when waiting for a long time or when dealing with problems or difficult people: done in a careful way over a long period of time without hurrying. (Merriam-Webster.com, 2011)*

Patience is the act of being patient. But, how do you remain calm and not become annoyed when storms rage and lives change and you are STILL waiting for resolution? How do you deal with difficult people or difficult situations that continue to hurt you and break? Let's just be real - being patient sucks. Being patient requires you to check your pride, and your agenda, at the door. Patience will require more of you than you are willing to give. When you mend a broken piece of pottery the glue takes time to dry. Patience allows you to really fix the broken pieces instead of making new cracks in your hurry to move ahead.

Look up Proverbs 19:11 and Ecclesiastes 7:8 in your favorite version of the Bible. Let's discover what the Bible says about how we can be more patient:

1. We embrace patience by overlooking offenses
In Proverbs 19:11, we are told it's to our glory to overlook an offense. What does that mean? The Hebrew word used is *tip'erot,* which means glory, splendor, or honor (Edward W. Goodrick, 2004). When you overlook an offense, when you forgive instead of remain bitter, you become a woman of honor and respect. That's exactly what a woman of God should be! The truth is, when you are waiting for restoration or a resolution you can almost guarantee you will be hurt again in the process. Forgive quickly and overlook an offense to develop patience.

2. We embrace patience by letting go of our pride
It is believed that King Solomon wrote the book of Ecclesiastes in the later part of his life. It is arguably one of the most negative books of the Bible on the surface. But it's tucked in the pages of this book that we find a very important step to developing patience - we let go of our pride. We have to get over the idea that we know better, would do something better, or would create a better outcome. Your pride will trip you up again and again. It will cause you to get annoyed quickly, rush ahead, and fix it in your own time and your own strength. This never works. Let go of pride so you can embrace patience.

"The end of a matter is better than its beginning..."
~Ecclesiastes 7:8

What a beautiful reminder from King Solomon about the storms in our lives. Better days are coming. Brokenness doesn't last forever.

SHE IS UNBROKEN...

Who comes to your mind when you think of a patient woman? How would you describe her?

Ask God to reveal any offenses or pride you need to overlook in your life. Write what He is telling you below:

DAY 13:

ACCEPTING THE SCARS

"Praise be to the God and Father of our Lord Jesus Christ, the Father of compassion and the God of all comfort, who comforts us in all our troubles, so that we can comfort those in any trouble with the comfort we ourselves receive from God." ~2 Corinthians 1:3-4

TRUTH STATEMENT®

I will embrace my scars and my story so I can spread hope and healing to others around me.

SHE EMBRACES THE CRACKS...

After a storm rages through our lives, we are left with broken pieces. When we choose to accept the process of restoration those wounds start to heal. Sometimes after a wound heals a scar remains. Scars are reminders. Sometimes scars are on the outside; but, more often than not, your scars will not be visible to the naked eye. Your deepest wounds are usually under the surface.

I can't tell you how many times I have people tell me, "I had no idea you were even struggling," or "I didn't realize your marriage was that broken," when they hear my story. When I look back at pictures during the worst seasons of my life I can see the light is gone from my eyes, but on the outside things looked OK. I didn't look sick. The truth is, when you look at someone who has overcome the odds, you will not always see the scars on her body. You will see her scars on her mind and her heart.

Scars remind us of why we are the way we are. They remind us of who we have been and the lessons we have learned on life's journey. They remind us of the things and people we've lost. They help us remember our courage and God's faithfulness. Scars are a reminder that even the deepest wounds eventually heal.

It's for this reason we have to embrace the cracks that are making us whole. We have to get really good at accepting every chapter of our story, even the dark ones, because this is how we comfort our sisters, mothers, daughters, and best friends. When we can share the truth about the scars in our lives we give another woman courage. When we bravely share our weaknesses, another woman finds the strength to take one step forward into the light. The Bible tells us to comfort those with the same compassion we have been comforted with. We can't do that if we can't embrace the scars left behind.

It's time to appreciate and celebrate those hard-earned battle wounds! Your scars are important. They are proof that we can all do hard things. Don't hide them. Don't pretend like they are not there. Embrace the scars. Embrace the healed areas of your life. Comfort others who are walking a similar path. Your scars are healing to those around you. Show them they are not alone and that someday they will have scars too, instead of gaping wounds.

SHE IS DETERMINED...

> *"My grace is enough; it's all you need. My strength comes into its own in your weakness. Once I heard that, I was glad to let it happen. I quit focusing on the handicap and began appreciating the gift. It was a case of Christ's strength moving in on my weakness. Now I take limitations in stride, and with good cheer, these limitations that cut me down to size—abuse, accidents, opposition, bad breaks. I just let Christ take over! And so the weaker I get, the stronger I become." ~2 Corinthians 12:9-10 (the Message)*

> ***Testimony**: Verb. Proof or evidence that something exists or is true. (Merriam-Webster.com, 2011)*

Your story is important. Giving testimony to what God has done in your life is powerful. Your vulnerability will inspire others. There are many verses in the Bible about embracing the broken pieces of your life and sharing what God has done for you. Take some time to look up the following verses. Jot down a few notes as you read each one. Focus on the power in embracing your scars and telling your story.

- Psalm 22:22

- Psalm 107:1-2

- Matthew 5:14-16

- Mark 5:19

- Philippians 1:12

- Revelation 12:11

SHE IS UNBROKEN...

Picture in your mind the deepest wound you have ever experienced. If another woman came to you suffering from the same thing, what would you tell her? How could your scars bring her hope? Write what you would say below:

What is God saying to you as you complete today's study?

DAY 14:

ACCEPTING THE WAITING

"I believe that I shall look upon the goodness of the LORD in the land of the living! Wait for the LORD; be strong, and let your heart take courage; wait for the LORD!" ~Psalm 27:13-14

TRUTH STATEMENT®

I am waiting in expectation for my new beginning.

SHE EMBRACES THE CRACKS...

Wait.

I'm not sure if there is any other word that makes me cringe like the word wait. It's just one of those words that makes me want to scream, "No. I will not!" And there is so much waiting when it comes to healing the broken pieces in our lives! We must wait for the timing to be right, for our raw emotions to settle, and for understanding and wisdom. We just have to wait, a lot!

Tucked in the pages of the Old Testament is the story of a nameless woman who had to wait a long time for God to fulfill a promise to her. You can find her story in the book of Judges Chapter 13. She was simply called "the wife of Menoah of Zorah" and was a very wealthy and honored woman. Menoah's wife was known as a woman who was very joyful… but also a woman of deep sorrow. She had everything the world deemed as worthy and honorable except the one thing she wanted… a child!

The thing I love about Menoah's wife is unlike some of the other barren women in the Bible, there is no record of her complaining or becoming impatient while she waited. God eventually answered her prayers for a child and she bore a son and named him Samson. Menoah's wife was faithful and joyful while waiting for God to give the child He promised… but many of her counterparts were bitter complainers. What was the difference?

I have to think it's because she refused to let anger, disappointment, doubt, or worry take hold in her heart while she waited for God to give her a child. I can imagine she felt these kinds of intense emotions - but she didn't stay stuck in them. That's the key. We can, and should, experience deep painful emotions when we are broken and waiting; but we cannot stay stuck in them. Waiting is one of the tools God uses to develop our character.

Don't let bitterness take root just because the season is lasting longer than you want. It rubs off your rough edges, wrong intentions, impatience, doubt, and brings you to a deeper faith and trust in the God who loves you the most.

SHE IS DETERMINED...

> ***Wait:*** *Verb. To remain in a state in which you expect or hope that something will happen soon. (Merriam-Webster.com, 2011)*

Wait. To remain. But how do you get through the waiting process when it seems like your new normal and your new future are taking eons to show up? Here are four steps to take while you are in a season of "Wait."

1. Ask for wisdom and understanding from God - God promises to give you wisdom if you will only ask. He promises to help you as you wait. You only need to be patient enough to listen and obey.

> *"If any of you lacks wisdom, let him ask God, who gives generously to all without reproach, and it will be given him."*
> *~James 1:5*

2. Seek Godly Counsel - When you are in a season of waiting you can get very weary. Weariness can lead to hasty decisions if you are not careful. Find a small group of people who can share your burdens and give you godly counsel while you wait.

> *"The way of a fool is right in his own eyes, but a wise man listens to advice." ~Proverbs 12:15*

3. Remind yourself of God's promises – Has God promised you something like he did Menoah's wife? While you are waiting for Him to fulfill that promise remind yourself of it often. Remind yourself of God's faithfulness. Remind your heart to be patient so you can receive the full blessing of a promise fulfilled in the right time.

> *"God is our refuge and strength, a very present help in trouble. Therefore we will not fear, though the earth should change and though the mountains slip into the heart of the sea; though its waters roar and foam, though the mountains quake at its swelling pride. Selah. The LORD of hosts is with us; the God of Jacob is our stronghold." ~Psalm 46:1-3, 7*

4. Surround yourself with truth – Doubt and fear will rear their ugly heads while you are in a season of waiting. It is your job to surround yourself with truth. Write out truth statements and post them everywhere. Find a worship song that speaks to your pain point, and gives you peace, and play it on repeat.

> *"Do not be conformed to this world, but be transformed by the renewal of your mind, that by testing you may discern what is the will of God, what is good and acceptable and perfect." ~Romans 12:2*

SHE IS UNBROKEN...

Which one of the four steps do you struggle with the most while you are waiting? Why?

How can you get better at that step in the future?

What is God saying to you as you complete today's study?

DAY 15:

THE PROMISE OF FREEDOM

"The Lord is close to the brokenhearted and saves those who are crushed in spirit." ~Psalm 34:18

TRUTH STATEMENT®

God is in control. His truth will set me free.

SHE EMBRACES THE CRACKS...

A few years ago I found myself in a storm of epic proportions. What started out as a dream job turned into a toxic situation where I found myself grasping desperately for my bearings as gale force winds raged around me. I wanted nothing more than to run away, lick my wounds, and quickly heal from this horrendous situation. But, the healing process was not going to be quick.

That storm caused emotional, mental, and spiritual wounds so deep it took years for them to heal. During that time I often asked God, "Why?" *Why did I have to walk through this storm? Why did they betray me? Why did it hurt so much? Why didn't telling the truth change anything?* I wanted to understand. I wanted to put the broken pieces back together. I wanted resolution, and I really wanted control. I wanted to control everything because I didn't want to be sad anymore. I needed to be free.

A few years later, I got the answer to those "why" questions. What God revealed to me one night while writing in my journal was something that completely changed my world. God showed me that sometimes telling the truth doesn't change the situation at all. Now stay with me here. That night, God reminded me that I had zero control over the situation and the outcome, no matter what I said or did. He was in control.

I used to think that speaking up to tell the truth would somehow bring freedom and healing and the storm would stop. Hello, ego trip.

God put me in my place and reminded me that it is His Truth that sets people free. Not mine. If freedom and healing were not happening, then it was because they were not ready, and He was working behind the scenes.

As I journaled through this new idea, God revealed even more. The truth might not have set them free, but it had set ME free. It had set me free from the lies that were spoken over me, from the rumors that were spread about me, from the condemnation I felt, and from feeling responsible for the outcome. The truth had set me free from the grip of the enemy. The truth set me free to be obedient and release the control back to God.

Before I went to bed that night, I wrote, "Be brave, little one. This might not end the way you want. But I'm in control." It's a promise I continue to cling to when dark storm clouds gather in my life. Maybe you need to cling to this promise today, too. Beautiful woman of God, be brave. This might not end the way you want. And that's ok. God is still in control.

SHE IS DETERMINED...

> *"To the Jews who had believed him, Jesus said, "If you hold to my teaching, you are really my disciples. Then you will know the truth, and the truth will set you free." ~John 8:31-32*

How often do we take a verse out of context and use it incorrectly because we don't fully understand the whole story? Way more than we probably realize if we are not careful. Today we are going to spend some time in John Chapter 8. This is the very chapter where we find the very popular saying, "You will know the truth and the truth will set you free." However, we will also discover that the freedom we are expecting might not be the same kind of freedom Jesus promises.

Look up John 8:12-59 and read the entire text. (If you have time, start from Verse 1 and read the entire chapter.)

Then go back and read it again. As you read it through the second time underline every time Jesus' word or character is questioned.

In this one short chapter, you find Jesus continually defending His character, His calling, His sanity, His work, His choices, and His words. Were you surprised by how often Jesus was questioned? I was! They simply did not believe the Son of God was telling the truth! Telling the truth did not change the situation at all for Jesus. We know this because, not long after this exchange, the same people would crucify Him. How much more can we assume that sometimes the truth will not change a situation at all for us? Sometimes telling the truth brings a different kind of freedom than we were expecting. But never doubt, child of God, the freedom you find will be worth it.

How did reading this passage of Scripture make you feel?

SHE IS UNBROKEN...

What are the things God has set you free from as a direct result of a storm you experienced in your life?

Be brave little one. This might not end the way you want. But I'm in control.
How does this phrase make you feel?

What is God saying to you as you complete today's study?

DAY 16:

THE PROMISE OF PROTECTION

"Because she loves me," says the Lord, "I will rescue her; I will protect her, for she acknowledges my name." ~Psalm 91:14

TRUTH STATEMENT®

I am protected by God. I have nothing to fear.

SHE EMBRACES THE CRACKS...

We might not spend a lot of time talking about it in daily conversation; but you dear friend, are surrounded by angels. One of the promises God gives us in the Bible is one of protection. According to Hebrews 1:14, God created angels to serve Him and work for our good. I think we will be amazed when we get to heaven and see all the times God sent angels to protect and intervene on our behalf, especially in the midst of our darkest seasons.

A few years ago, I'm quite certain my then five-month-old daughter was entertaining angels in her bedroom. I had just finished listening to a podcast from Steven Furtick, the lead pastor at Elevation Church, and I was getting ready to turn out the lights when I heard a strange noise from the baby room. She had been sound asleep for hours, and usually slept through the night, so I was surprised to hear her! I got up out of bed, walked out into the hallway, and started to head to the kitchen to prep her bottle. However, I stopped short.

She wasn't crying. She was shrieking with glee! I snuck over to her bedroom door and listened. She was shrieking, cooing, giggling, and talking as loud and as fast as she could. In that dark nursery in the middle of the night, she was carrying on like her best friend was right next to her and she just had to spill all the details of her day. All I could think was that she was entertaining angels and I better not disturb them. I stood by her door and quietly listened to her conversation. I did not want to interrupt the heavenly exchange that was happening in her room.

This conversation continued for nearly 15 minutes. It stopped as quickly as it started. No crying, fussing, or complaining. She just got quiet and went back to sleep. I truly believe we are surrounded by heavenly beings and my daughter was talking to her guardian angel that night. It was one of the coolest things I have ever witnessed.

May we never forget the beautiful promises of protection given to us in God's Word. All of Heaven knows your name and is working towards your ultimate restoration and healing.

SHE IS DETERMINED...

The night Jesus was betrayed he spent hours praying in the Garden of Gethsemane. What you might not realize is one of the prayers that is recorded is one Jesus prayed for you. Before He died on the cross, Jesus asked His Father to protect those who love Him and believe in Him as well as the ones who would come to know Him through their testimony. (That's you!) Read the prayer below:

> *"I pray for them. I am not praying for the world, but for those you have given me, for they are yours. All I have is yours, and all you have is mine. And glory has come to me through them. I will remain in the world no longer, but they are still in the world, and I am coming to you. Holy Father, protect them by the power of your name, the name you gave me, so that they may be one as we are one.*
>
> *While I was with them, I protected them and kept them safe by that name you gave me. None has been lost except the one doomed to destruction so that Scripture would be fulfilled. I am coming to you now, but I say these things while I am still in the world, so that they may have the full measure of my joy within them.*
>
> *I have given them your word and the world has hated them, for they are not of the world any more than I am of the world. My prayer is not that you take them out of the world but that you protect them from*

the evil one.

They are not of the world, even as I am not of it. Sanctify them by the truth; your word is truth. As you sent me into the world, I have sent them into the world. For them I sanctify myself, that they too may be truly sanctified.

My prayer is not for them alone. I pray also for those who will believe in me through their message." ~John 17:13-20

How does the fact that Jesus prayed for your protection from every kind of evil before you were even born make you feel?

SHE IS UNBROKEN...

Describe a time in your life when God protected you in the midst of a storm:

Look up Psalm 91:11-12 and write it below:

What is God saying to you as you complete today's study?

DAY 17:

THE PROMISE OF FAITH

"Go," said Jesus, "your faith has healed you." Immediately he received his sight and followed Jesus along the road." ~Mark 10:52

TRUTH STATEMENT®

I am a woman of bondage-breaking faith.

SHE EMBRACES THE CRACKS...

My best friend and business partner, Mandy, was born with cystic fibrosis. CF is "a genetic disorder that affects mostly the lungs but also the pancreas, liver, kidneys, and intestine. Long-term issues include difficulty breathing and coughing up mucus as a result of frequent lung infections." (Wikipedia, n.d.) She is a constant example to me of a woman who has embraced the cracks in her life and found wholeness, strength, and unbreakable faith.

In her book, *She Who Overcomes*, Mandy shares how she rose up from the ashes in her life and overcame obstacles that many thought were impossible for her to accomplish. In chapter eight, Mandy shares her story of healing and walking by faith. What started as a divine season of healing from the symptoms of CF ended with her fighting for her life. In March of 2012, at 93 lbs and 22% lung function, she entered the hospital for 22 days. There were times when we were not sure she would walk out again. It was during that season, when she was literally fighting for her life and desperately holding on to her fragile faith, that she wrote this letter:

> *My child,*
>
> *We will work through this together. I will not abandon you nor will I destroy you...this will not destroy you. Just as a seed has to die before it sprouts, you are dying to old destructive thought patterns and being molded by truth. You have bondage breaking faith, boldness, and courage to face painful things for my glory. I gave you that boldness. I gave you that courage...I*

> *gave you that faith. For a long time it has been trampled on but it's better to trust in the Lord than to trust in man - even if that means trusting God over your loved ones. This is the time to trust me fully. Seek me with all of your heart and all of your mind and all your soul and you will find me. My promises are true. I will never leave you nor forsake you. I will not make you feel guilty or manipulate you or try to control you. I will listen to you, love you, console you, renew you, and guide you. I will carry you through this.*
>
> *I am the Lord Almighty - is anything too hard for me?* (Anderson, 2016)

I want a faith like that, don't you? A faith that looks for His Face in the midst of chaos and pain. A faith that trusts that God is working even when you are fighting for your life with every breath that you have. A faith that even in the darkness can still hear God's still voice whisper in her soul, "I'm here. Is anything too hard for me?"

SHE IS DETERMINED...

> *"I see what you've done. Now see what I've done. I've opened a door before you that no one can slam shut. You don't have much strength, I know that; you used what you had to keep my Word. You didn't deny me when times were rough." ~Revelation 3:8-11*

Bondage-breaking faith looks crazy to those who are not walking the same path as you. Trust me when I say that lots of people thought Mandy had completely lost her senses and shook their heads in disbelief and what they thought was completely naive faith. But, faith is being sure of what you hope for and confident of what you do not see no matter what anyone else says or thinks. (Hebrews 11:1)

Your faith is a blessing from God! It is the anchor you hold on to when the storms of life rage around you. Listed below are beautiful promises of blessing for anyone who can hold on to their faith in the midst of life's biggest struggles. As you look up each verse, or verses, take some time to jot down what these words mean to you.

- Proverbs 3:3-4

- Luke 1:37

- Romans 12:12

- Galatians 6:9

SHE IS UNBROKEN...

How did reading Mandy's story, and the letter she wrote, make you feel about embracing a deeper level of faith?

Is there a "door" that God has opened in your life that you need to walk through by faith? What is stopping you?

What is God saying to you as you complete today's study?

DAY 18:
THE PROMISE OF BLESSINGS

"For out of His fullness [the superabundance of His grace and truth] we have all received grace upon grace [spiritual blessing upon spiritual blessing, favor upon favor, and gift heaped upon gift]." ~John 1:16 (AMP)

TRUTH STATEMENT®

I am blessed with every spiritual blessing. I will pray with confidence because of God's amazing grace towards me.

SHE EMBRACES THE CRACKS...

When you walk through brokenness, your vision gets cloudy to the blessings in your life. The Bible is full of promises of blessings from God: material blessings, spiritual blessings, blessings on earth, blessings in Heaven. You are promised incredible blessings. In fact, the Bible promises you overflowing blessings! God says He will give you blessings and they will be abundant.

"My cup overflows with blessings." ~*Psalm 23:5*

The image of an overflowing cup was a very powerful symbol in the ancient world. Hosts would use the cup as a way of sending a message to their guests. If the cup stayed full, a guest would know that he was welcome to continue the visit. If, however, the cup was left empty, it was a sign that it was getting late and the guest should prepare to leave.

If the host really enjoyed his guest's company, he would fill the cup until it overflowed and the liquid ran down the table. Isn't that amazing? David is telling us in Psalm 23, that God enjoys blessing us so much that He can't help but let our cup overflow. Such a beautiful visual of the God we serve.

Two of the blessings we are going to focus on for today are the blessing of prayer and the blessing of grace. We have a direct line of communication with God through prayer. It is an incredible blessing and an incredible weapon if we will only use it. The dictionary defines grace as "unmerited divine assistance." (Merriam-Webster.com, 2011) My favorite definition of grace is this quote:

> *"Grace means that all of your mistakes now serve a purpose instead of serving shame." ~Unknown*

Now, let me ask you a question. How wet is your table? Do you look around and see cups half full, empty, or overflowing? God wants your cup to overflow. But you have to be willing to receive it. Unclench your fists and open up your hands to accept the blessings. He wants to bless you richly and desires you to know the fullness of His grace. Broken vessels cannot hold everything God wants to pour into your life.

SHE IS DETERMINED...

The Blessing of Prayer

Look up these verses on prayer in the Bible. Take a moment to jot down your thoughts as you read each verse.

- Jeremiah 29:19

- Psalm 17:6

- Romans 8:26

The Bible is a book of prayers. In fact, there are over 660 recorded prayers in the Bible! God wants you to take the blessing of prayer seriously. Prayer is an incredibly powerful blessing. It changes your life and it changes the lives of the people you have a privilege to pray for. It is the only way for us to communicate with God; and we are promised that He hears us when we call, understands when we have no words, and is near.

The Blessing of Grace:
Look up these verses on grace in the Bible. Take a moment to jot down your thoughts as you read each verse.

- Romans 6:14

- Ephesians 4:7

- Hebrews 4:16

Grace means that there is nothing we can do to make God love us more and there is nothing we can do to make God love us less. God's grace and love are blessings we cannot earn and we do not deserve. Grace also means sin no longer has dominion over us! We can approach our God with confidence in our times of need because of the blessing of grace.

SHE IS UNBROKEN...

Use the space below to write out a prayer to God about the brokenness you are trying to embrace. Thank Him for the gift of His grace and the blessings you can see in the mess.

Dear God,

Date: ____________________

DAY 19:
THE PROMISE OF UNDERSTANDING

"If you love me, keep my commands. And I will ask the Father, and he will give you another advocate to help you and be with you forever—the Spirit of truth. The world cannot accept him because it neither sees him nor knows him."
~John 14:15-16

TRUTH STATEMENT®

I can act with wisdom, understanding, knowledge, and courage because of the Holy Spirit who dwells in me.

SHE EMBRACES THE CRACKS...

Aren't you grateful for the promise that one day you will fully understand the pain and the suffering you have experienced? I am! The big questions we seem to ask when it comes to understanding are *how*, *what*, and *when*.

Let's tackle the *how* first. The Holy Spirit gives us the ability to understand; that is *how* we are able to. Simply put, the Holy Spirit is the third person of the trinity: God the Father, God the Son, and God the Spirit. He dwells inside every person who has accepted Christ as their Savior and guides them as they grow in spiritual maturity. Cool!

Next, the *what.* Sometimes we take verses like John 13:7 that say, "You do not realize now what I am doing, but later you will understand," and pull them out of context and apply them to this situation or that situation. We do it to bring hope to a hopeless circumstance with the promise that someday we will understand. Taken out of context, it provides false hope and unrealistic expectations.

In this section of Scripture, Jesus is getting ready to wash the disciples feet and Peter doesn't understand why Jesus is doing this. Jesus tells Peter that he will eventually understand. Eventually comes a few verses down when Jesus explains to all the disciples that washing their feet is an example of the kind of servants He expects them to be to others.

The truth is, there will be many dark seasons in your life where there will be more questions than answers. That's OK. The amazing thing we *do* get to understand, thanks to the Holy Spirit, is God. We get to know and understand things about our Heavenly Father that seem impossible. We get to know Him like we get to know our best friend. That is the beautiful promise of understanding we cling to. And, because we are created in His image, we get to know things about ourselves as well. We get to understand on a deeper level our motives, our decisions, our instincts, and our impulses.

Finally, the *when*. There is an old saying that hindsight is 20/20. When it comes to understanding, our hindsight could come quickly or it could come when we cross into Heaven. God doesn't give us the answer to the *when* question very often because He wants us to trust Him and not rush the process.

SHE IS DETERMINED...

Look up and read Isaiah 11:1-3

Based on the Messianic Prophecy (a promise of Jesus) you just read there are seven different ways the Holy Spirit operates. These are different than the gifts of the Holy Spirit listed in I Corinthians 12 where every believer is given a gift like faith, healing, discernment, etc. These seven characteristics describe the Holy Spirit and better help us understand how it guides and comforts us: Wisdom, understanding, counsel, power, knowledge, and awe. Let's break them down.

Wisdom- The Hebrew word for wisdom used in this verse means, "wisdom, skill, learning; this can refer to skill in life, trade, war, or spiritual things." (Edward W. Goodrick, 2004) The dictionary defines wisdom as, "the ability to discern or judge what is true, right, or lasting." (Merriam-Webster.com, 2011)

Understanding- The Catechism of the Catholic Church explains understanding like this,

> "*In understanding, we comprehend how we need to live as followers of Christ. A person with understanding is not confused by the conflicting messages in our culture about the right way to live. The gift of understanding perfects a person's speculative reason in the apprehension of truth. It is the gift whereby self-evident principles are known.*" (Church)

Counsel- The Hebrew word for counsel in this verse is *esa,* defined as "advice, counsel, plan, purpose, scheme." (Edward W. Goodrick, 2004) This means that the Holy Spirit can help you know which choice to make when you are faced with a decision.

Power- The Hebrew word for power in this verse is *gebura* which means, "power, strength, might, achievement, mighty acts, and source of strength." (Edward W. Goodrick, 2004) This is where we find our courage and strength to do the hard things!

Knowledge- The dictionary defines knowledge as, "information, understanding, or skill that you get from experience or education; awareness of something; the state of being aware of something." (Merriam-Webster.com, 2011) Knowledge can exist without wisdom - but not the other way around. The Holy Spirit can help us be wise *and* have knowledge.

Fear of the Lord (Awe)- The fear of the Lord means we understand the glory and majesty of our God. The Holy Spirit helps us to understand this fear! The fear of the Lord prolongs our life (Proverbs 10:27), brings riches and honor (Proverbs 22:4), brings God's favor (Psalm 147:11), and even lets you sleep in peace (Proverbs 19:23).

SHE IS UNBROKEN...

In your own words, how would you explain the promise of understanding?

What are some ways you can start developing a deeper relationship with the Holy Spirit and access the characteristics of wisdom, understanding, counsel, power, knowledge, and the fear of the Lord?

What is God saying to you as you complete today's study?

DAY 20:

THE PROMISE OF RESTORATION

"The Lord says, "I will give you back what you have lost to the locusts…and you will praise the Lord your God who does this miracle for you. Never again will my people be disappointed." ~Joel 2:25-26

TRUTH STATEMENT®

My life is being restored. God promises to give back what the enemy stole from me!

SHE EMBRACES THE CRACKS...

One day I was looking out the patio door over our backyard and I started to get a little emotional. If you had been standing beside me you would have seen a large yard without a porch, without a fence, and without any trees or rocks or flowers. There was, however, a beautiful large hill covered with baby grass sprouts. It probably wouldn't have looked like much to you. It was certainly not in the running for a *Better Homes and Gardens* cover. But to me that baby grass was proof of restoration.

If I'm unhappy, I try to change my environment first. It's a horrible pattern. Maybe you can relate? When I was growing up, my family moved more times than I can count on two hands. I was raised to move on. Don't get too comfortable. Don't put down roots. If you are not happy, change your environment. It was a pattern I found myself repeating with my own family every few years.

That baby grass growing in our backyard was proof that I was learning how to stay in one place long enough to put down roots.

Instead of letting our house sell and dropping a huge mansion in our lap where our children would have their own rooms and our guests could be entertained easily, God taught me a lesson. He let me experience what it felt like to change my heart first - and not my environment. He was gracious and saved us from financial ruin when six months later our finances changed drastically and He started softening my heart towards the home I have grown to love. He let me see what happens when you stay.

As I write this, my husband and I will celebrate 14 years of marriage in a few months. This is the first spring we have a yard with grass. The new baby grass is a sign of the promise. God works in mysterious ways and while growing grass probably isn't a miracle, making my heart content and happy in a dream that didn't go the way I planned is. I've learned that the promise of restoration is worth every painful crack and storm it took to get here.

Beginnings should be celebrated. Promises should be remembered. And, I am going to celebrate as I watch this yard go from tiny grass seeds to beautiful sanctuary. So grow, little grass… we've got big plans for you.

SHE IS DETERMINED...

> ***Restoration:*** *Noun. The act or process of returning something to its original condition by repairing it, cleaning it, etc.; the act of bringing back something that existed before : the act of returning something that was stolen or taken. (Merriam-Webster.com, 2011)*

Today, we are going to explore the life of Job in the Old Testament. Job was a man who understood the process of restoration, as we will see as we study his life.

Read Job 1:1-3

Write Job's blessing listed in this first passage:

What was Job known as?

Read Job 1:9, 1:13-19, 2:7-8

What does Satan steal from Job, and afflict him with, in an attempt to make him curse God?

Read Job 1:12, 2:6, Chapters 40-42

What is God's response to Job's suffering to Satan and to Job himself?

Read Job 42:1-16

What did God restore for Job?

**Extra credit! Read the exchange of Job and his friends (it's literally the whole book, almost!) Take notes on the different ways they all respond to Job's storm.*

SHE IS UNBROKEN...

What is the biggest insight you've gained from studying Job's life?

In what areas of your life has God already brought restoration?

What is God saying to you as you complete today's study?

DAY 21:

THE PROMISE OF SOMETHING NEW

"Behold, the former things have come to pass, and new things I now declare; before they spring forth, I tell you of them." ~Isaiah 42:9

TRUTH STATEMENT®

I am confident in the promise that God is doing a new thing in my life.

SHE EMBRACES THE CRACKS...

There is nothing like breathing in the crisp clean air after a summer rainstorm. It's intoxicating in its freshness! You can only smell the air in that wonderful aroma after a storm. It's so wonderful that perfumers have been trying to mimic and bottle the scent for centuries. You cannot smell it before the storm, and only faintly during, but you really smell it after. Some things are worth the wait.

To me, this is a beautiful reminder that after the storm rages in my life, there will always be beauty and restoration on the other side of pain. Not only does God promise to restore what was lost, He also promises to do a NEW thing.

> *"A woman does not give birth before she feels the pain. A woman must feel the pain of childbirth before she can see the boy she gives birth too. Who ever heard of such a thing? In the same way, no one ever saw a new world begin in one day. No one has ever heard of a new nation that began in one day. But when Zion feels the pain, she will give birth to her children. In the same way, I will not cause pain without allowing something new to be born."* ~Isaiah 66:7-9

This is a promise I cling to when storms rage in my life. God will always use the pain in my life to bring forth something good. He will not cause pain in my life without allowing it to bring something new. I've got three gorgeous children in my house, and I understand that sometimes pain brings the most beautiful blessings. The birthing process is painful!

> *"We've all heard that when God closes a door, He opens a window. But keep on the lookout for unexpected options. Like a skylight. Or a ventilation shaft. Or a mouse hole, a chimney flue, or corroded dry wall that you can easily knock down with a head-butt. We just have to recognize opportunities. Situations that initially look disastrous can often turn out to be blessings." ~Sean Dillion* (Dillion)

While you are waiting for restoration and the new thing in your life, your job is to look for the opportunities that God is opening up for you. I love this quote from Sean Dillion because it beautifully illustrates what we should be looking for! We can't look for signs we recognized in the past. We have to look with new eyes. If we don't, we will miss the new thing because it didn't look like we expected it to.

SHE IS DETERMINED...

Below, you will find different verses that talk about the promise of something new in your life. In the space provided, write down each verse. You can also use the space to write down notes about what you are learning about this promise of something new being brought from pain.

- Isaiah 43:19

- Isaiah 62:2

- Isaiah 65:17

- Romans 5:6

- 2 Corinthians 5:17

- Revelation 21:5

SHE IS UNBROKEN...

Describe a time you have experienced God do a new thing in your life after a storm:

What did you learn about the promise of something new from the verses you studied in the previous section?

What is God saying to you as you complete today's study?

DAY 22:

FINDING JOY

"Those who sow with tears will reap with songs of joy. Those who go out weeping, carrying seed to sow, will return with songs of joy, carrying sheaves with them." ~Psalm 126:5-6

TRUTH STATEMENT®

I am content. My soul is secure. I am joyful.

SHE EMBRACES THE CRACKS...

For the next seven days, we'll be focusing on how we can acquire the very attributes we need to make the right choices, to accept our broken pieces and our scars, and to lean on the promises when storms rage in our lives. What are the best ways to embrace the broken pieces and find healing and wholeness? The secrets are in the character qualities listed in Galatians 5:22-23 - love, joy, peace, patience, kindness, goodness, faithfulness, gentleness, and self-control. (i.e. - the fruits of the spirit!) Today we begin with joy.

> *"But the fruit of the Spirit is love, joy, peace, patience, kindness, goodness, faithfulness, gentleness and self-control. Against such things there is no law." ~Galatians 5:22-23*

I think we have this misconception about what joy really means. For some reason I think we get stuck on the idea that joy equals happy. It doesn't. But, how in the world are we supposed to be happy about horrible storms, ruined lives, and broken pieces? We aren't. Joy means a lot more than we realize! Part of the definition of joy is actually, "a feeling of great happiness." But did you know that happy and happiness do not mean the same thing?

> ***Happy**: Adjective. Feeling pleasure and enjoyment because of your life, situation, etc. (Merriam-Webster.com, 2011)*

> ***Happiness**: Noun. A state of well-being or contentment. Joy. (Merriam-Webster.com, 2011)*

Joy is not a sticky sweet emotion that you spill all over everyone as you skip down the road completely clueless to the trials and difficulties around you. When you look at the definitions of happy and happiness, you can see the difference! Joy does not mean you deny anger, hurt, and sadness when the situations in your life get too tough to handle. Joy means you are content and well in your soul despite your circumstances.

Joy is something you are. You will either choose to be joyful or you will not. Happiness comes down to your choices. Finding your joy means you choose to have a good attitude when others around you don't. Finding your joy means you rejoice because God is good even when your circumstances are not. Finding your joy means you are content because you know God is in control and is going to do something great in your life. Finding your joy brings the contentment you need to truly embrace the cracks that are making you whole.

SHE IS DETERMINED...

> ***Joy:*** *Noun. A feeling of great happiness. a source or cause of great happiness: something or someone that gives joy to someone. (Merriam-Webster.com, 2011)*

The word *joy* is mentioned over 200 times in the Bible! Some Greek words for joy are verbs but not in Galatians 5:22. It's a noun. Why is that interesting? Because a verb indicates action and a noun is something you have or are. When Paul writes the fruit of the Spirit is Joy, he means you should BE joy, not just act joyful. But, how do we do that? How do we become more content in the midst of obstacles and pain? Thankfully, Jesus gives us a model to follow in how to cultivate this feeling of contentment and ease despite our circumstances.

1. Stay connected to the Father- Jesus was in constant relationship with His Heavenly Father. He practiced spiritual disciplines like reading the Word and praying even in His most difficult seasons. He spent hours in prayer the night before He was betrayed! You can do no less. This is not a time issue. This is a power issue. You have to stay plugged in to your power source to let HIM start to change your thoughts, attitudes, and behaviors to joy instead of discontentment. (See Matthew 26:36-46)

2. Practice gratitude- When Jesus prayed, He always gave thanks to His Father. Gratitude takes the focus off of your immediate problems and helps you focus on your blessings instead. Being grateful allows you to experience pain, grief, anger, and disappointment in a healthy way instead of letting bitterness take root. If Jesus practiced gratitude, we need to do the same to cultivate the spirit of joy. (See John 11:41-42)

3. Give of yourself to others- Brokenness can make you weary and tired and want to just take a nap and shut out the world. Even Jesus felt this way sometimes, but He knew how to juggle weariness and the needs of those around Him. He took breaks when He needed to but He didn't shut down and turn away when faced with people who needed Him. You have to do the same thing! Take the focus off of you and your problems once in a while and focus on someone else. The more outside your comfort zone the better. There are hundreds of ways to give to someone else, you just have use your imagination. (See Matthew 14:13-14)

SHE IS UNBROKEN...

What are specific things you can do this week to stay connected to God, or be more grateful, so you can acquire more joy in your life?

What are five things you could do to give back to others in the next two weeks? Write them below:

What is God saying to you as you complete today's study?

DAY 23:
FINDING LOVE

"So this is my prayer: that your love will flourish and that you will not only love much but well. Learn to love appropriately. You need to use your head and test your feelings so that your love is sincere and intelligent, not sentimental gush. Live a lover's life, circumspect and exemplary, a life Jesus will be proud of: bountiful in fruits from the soul, making Jesus Christ attractive to all, getting everyone involved in the glory and praise of God."

~Philippians 1:9-11 (the Message)

TRUTH STATEMENT®

I will make sacrifices, so my love is sincere. I will love in a way that makes Jesus proud.

SHE EMBRACES THE CRACKS...

> *"But the fruit of the Spirit is love, joy, peace, patience, kindness, goodness, faithfulness, gentleness and self-control. Against such things there is no law." ~Galatians 5:22-23*

Galatians is one of the books of the Bible written by the apostle Paul. It is a letter written directly to the church in Galatia. The whole purpose of the letter was to address a growing issue in the church of wanting to combine legalism with grace. The book of Galatians is Paul reminding the young church in Galatia that you can only be saved through faith in Jesus alone. It is a book about freedom! It is in this letter, in this context, that you find Paul writing about the "Fruits of the Spirit."

Like the entire New Testament, the book of Galatians was written in Greek. The Greek language has many different words to explain the meaning of love. The word *love* in Galatians 5:22 is the Greek word *agape,* which is described as a sacrificial love. It is a love that is very different from romantic love or deep friendship. This is the kind of love God uses to describe Himself! It is His very nature and character! God sacrificed His own Son to die for our sins because He loved us that much. He expects us to love each other the same way.

If I'm being honest, I have a hard time with this kind of love. Agape love isn't my first instinct when I'm dealing with broken pieces in my life. My first instinct is, "Show me you are worthy and trustworthy and then maybe you will earn that kind of love." It's incredibly difficult for me to not build up the wall I've spent years knocking down when someone I trusted hurts me. Maybe you understand exactly what I'm talking about. This kind of love is hard!

Sacrificial love demands that you put your guard down and trust others. Sacrificial love demands that you give more than you receive. Sacrificial love demands that you forgive an enemy *and a* friend. And let's just be real, sometimes the latter is harder than the former! A sacrificial love will force you to treat others better than they treat you. Sacrificial love demands that you heal the broken pieces and find restoration, without waiting for an apology. Sacrificial love means that you have to trust the One who can bring true healing, God.

The best things in life are the ones that cost you something… and that includes love.

SHE IS DETERMINED…

> ***Agape:*** *Greek. Noun. The active love of God for His Son and His people, and the active love His people are to have for God, each other, and even enemies. (Merriam-Webster.com, 2011)*

Agape love is kind, patient, protective, and hopeful. It is not hateful, revengeful, or bitter. When you feel the anger start to rise inside you and you want to act selfish and mean, choose love instead. Know why? Because… love looks good on you, beautiful lady! It makes you look more and more like your heavenly Father. Let's spend some time looking at what the Bible says about sacrificial love.

Look up each one of the following verses and record what you learn as you dig deeper in the meaning of the word agape:

- Matthew 5:44

- John 15:9-19 *(note: every time the word love is mentioned in this passage it is the same sacrificial meaning as agape except for the word love in verse 19)*

- Romans 12:9

- I Corinthians 8:1

- 2 Timothy 1:7

- I John 4:7-21

SHE IS UNBROKEN...

What are some ways you can demonstrate agape love to someone who has hurt you?

Write down the Bible verse that meant the most to you from the previous section:

What is God saying to you as you complete today's study?

DAY 24:
FINDING PEACE

"I'm leaving you well and whole. That's my parting gift to you. Peace. I don't leave you the way you're used to being left-feeling abandoned, bereft. So don't be upset. Don't be distraught." ~John 14:27 (the Message)

TRUTH STATEMENT®

My heart and mind are at peace. I have no reason to worry or fear.

SHE EMBRACES THE CRACKS...

I love the word "Peace," don't you? It's one of those words that makes you want to take a deep breath, breathe it out slowly, and just relax. It instantly takes me away to quiet moments spent alone after the kiddos are in bed for the night. Or, in my dreams, to a sandy white beach by the ocean where I am sipping fruity drinks with straws in them and doing nothing but soaking up the sun. No troubles, no burdens, no deadlines, no agenda...just peace.

The word peace has a lot of different meanings. My two favorite definitions are "*a state of tranquility or quiet,*" and "*freedom from disquieting or oppressive thoughts or emotions.*" (Merriam-Webster.com, 2011) Did that last meaning sound familiar? It should. It is the exact opposite of the definition of worry we discussed on day six.

You are probably thinking, "Tranquility, quiet, freedom... give me more of that!!" I am too some days! Tranquility, quiet, and freedom can seem impossible when you have a household full of young children. Or you are a busy career woman climbing the corporate ladder. These two things don't equate "Peace" in my mind. I'm sure they don't for you either.

What God has taught me is that I can create tranquility, quiet, and freedom in my heart and soul no matter my circumstances. I can find tranquility even when my life is chaotic. God promises me peace and quiet when worry floods my mind. However, it's up to me to co-create this environment. It's up to me to tap into this promise of peace. It's up to me to create a space for peace in my life, in my mind, in my home, and in my soul.

God has given each one of us the gift of peace. We just need to learn to open it. You can have peace in the midst of chaos. You can find peace in the midst of crisis. You can find calm in the raging winds. You can have peace in the midst of screaming babies, looming deadlines, and rush hour traffic. You can experience freedom from oppressive and disquieting thoughts. You can! It's time to open the gift of peace and take a deep breath.

SHE IS DETERMINED...

There are two ways I consistently create peace in my life and home when I'm walking through painful seasons. The first is purposely creating peaceful spaces in my home and the second is to allow the worry to have a voice. Let's explore a little more about what that means.

> *"As water reflects the face, so one's life reflects the heart."*
> *~Proverbs 27:19*

Did you know your environment reflects the condition of your heart? I often joke about my seasons of depression and postpartum as my "Brown Period." I wore a lot of brown, my home was decorated in brown and beiges, and it just seemed to permeate every area of my life. There was no color in my life during the brown period. I was feeling dead on the inside and it showed in my environment. Over the last few years, I have been slowly replacing all the brown with color that reflects the joy and peace I've found from God healing my broken pieces.

One of my favorite things to do when I feel like there is a war raging inside my head is curl up in one of the peaceful nooks in my house.

I've always enjoyed little spaces in my home where I can read, relax, and 'introvert'. (There were none of these in the brown period.) I think it goes back to my dad creating a window seat in our back entry that I used as my nook when I was a little girl.

Do you have a quiet spot in your home where you can just rest and be? No kids allowed, just you and Jesus? If you don't it's time to find one, today.

> *"Do not be anxious about anything, but in every situation, by prayer and petition, with thanksgiving, present your requests to God. And the peace of God, which transcends all understanding, will guard your hearts and your minds in Christ Jesus." ~Philippians 4:6-7*

When worries flood into your heart and soul and threaten to torment, you have two choices: Let them stay in your brain and fester until you are completely paralyzed with fear; or let those worries have a voice. One of the beautiful things about creating a peaceful spot in your house is it's the perfect place for you to bring those worries to God. Maybe you need to write them out in a letter. Maybe you just need to read your Bible, or listen to worship music. Or maybe you need to say them out loud. Yes, I know how terrifying that sounds. But something I've learned from experiencing PPOCD is the anxious thoughts absolutely cannot stay in your head.

When you create a peaceful space in your home, you create a safe place to give your worries and anxious thoughts to the only One who can give you real peace.

SHE IS UNBROKEN...

If your environment reflects the condition of your heart, what are your surroundings saying? What would you like them to say?

What are some ways you can create more peace in your life and home?

What is God saying to you as you complete today's study?

DAY 25:

FINDING KINDNESS

"Do not let kindness and truth leave you; Bind them around your neck, Write them on the tablet of your heart." ~Proverbs 3:3

TRUTH STATEMENT®

Because God is kind to me, I will be kind to others.

SHE EMBRACES THE CRACKS...

When I am walking through storms and painful seasons in my life, I can act anything but kind. It's true. If you are anything like me, brokenness tends to make you extra-cranky not extra-loving. *Sigh.* That is not how God wants us to react though. He wants His children to be kind.

> *"Patience avoids a problem; kindness creates a blessing. One is preventative, the other proactive." ~Alex Kendrick (Kendrick, 2013)*

Kindness makes you into someone that others want to be around. Choosing to be kind is a blessing to those around you! One of the kindest women I've ever met is my friend, Darika. I've never heard this woman say a mean word about anyone. Even when she talks about the hard things in her life she remains kind and considerate. She goes out of her way to do kind things for others. She is one of those beautiful souls who only wants to see others blessed with no recognition for herself. She is loving and thoughtful and everything I aspire to be when it comes to kindness.

It has been said that kindness is love in action. Kind people are the best people to be around! I bet you can think of kind women, like Darika, in your own life. I am so grateful for women, and men, who continually teach me what kindness really looks like. There is such power in being kind! There is even an entire movement dedicated to practicing being kind called "Random Acts of Kindness." You've probably heard of random acts of kindness, or even done some of your own!

God says that if we are his daughters we will grow the fruit of kindness in our lives. Being kind shouldn't be a struggle. It should be a natural response of a life rooted in God. But let's be real… for many of us it is a struggle! We are all human and we all struggle with human emotions like anger, bitterness, jealousy, and loss. It can be extremely difficult to be kind when you are in the midst of brokenness. But it's not impossible.

If being kind is something you sometimes struggle with, it's time to examine your heart and mind to dig out the root of unkindness. Let's let God slowly polish those rough edges and heal those broken pieces so He can fill you up with kindness to overflowing.

SHE IS DETERMINED…

Kindness: *Noun. The quality or state of being kind. Synonyms: courtesy, grace, indulgence, favor, mercy, service. (Merriam-Webster.com, 2011)*

Kind: *Noun. Fundamental nature or quality. Synonyms: attentive, considerate, thoughtful. (Merriam-Webster.com, 2011)*

Look up each of the verses below and record what you learn as you dig deeper into the meaning of the word kindness and how it should appear in your life:

- I Corinthians 13:4

- Ephesians 4:32

- Colossians 3:12-14

Ask God to reveal any areas of unkindness in your own life. Ask Him to expose the real issue of why you struggle. Record what He is telling you below:

SHE IS UNBROKEN...

Write a list of 10 ways you can show kindness and be a blessing to someone else in the next 30 days:

1.

2.

3.

4.

5.

6.

7.

8.

9.

10.

DAY 26:

FINDING GOODNESS

"Love must be sincere. Hate what is evil; cling to what is good."
~Romans 12:9

TRUTH STATEMENT®

I am a good, strong, and hopeful woman. I will call out the goodness in myself and others around me.

SHE EMBRACES THE CRACKS...

As I pen this Bible Study, I am surrounded by reminders of a world largely living in fear. On July 7th, 2016, I wrote this on our company's Facebook page.

> *I can't sleep. I'm in tears.*
>
> *All I can do is throw my hands up and say ENOUGH! It needs to stop. We are a country hemorrhaging because of racism and intolerance, fear, and generational wounds.*
>
> *We can't stay silent anymore. We can't turn a blind eye anymore. Jesus was not silent about social and racial injustice and I sure as hell won't be silent either.*
>
> *I don't have the answers to fix this awful mess. But I do know we need to be women of prayer AND action to turn things around. We stand in the gap. We speak truth. We don't turn away. We acknowledge our own prejudices. We mourn for every life lost because of hate. We ask for forgiveness. We start in our own homes. We start tonight, even if all we do is lift our voices to say "We see you and we weep with you."*
>
> *- Raychel*

You have to look for goodness sometimes. It won't always be evident on the surface. Especially when you are reeling from a recent heartbreak or shocking event. But it's there. There is still goodness.

There are still good things to celebrate. There are still good things to call out in one another. God wants us to weep with those who weep, demand justice for those whose voices are silenced, and shine a light of goodness and hope in the darkness.

> *"When I was a boy and I would see scary things in the news, my mother would say to me, "Look for the helpers. You will always find people who are helping." ~Fred Rogers*

When we grow the fruit of goodness in our lives, we will seek answers to the tough questions, we will get our hands dirty, we will be instruments of peace and reconciliation, and we will help those who cannot help themselves. That's what goodness looks like. When chaos is raging, people will look for the helpers. They will look for those who are doing good in the midst of pain. We need goodness to rise up in the midst of brokenness and pain.

SHE IS DETERMINED...

> ***Goodness:*** *Noun. The quality or state of being good. Excellence of morals and behavior. Synonyms: character, decency, morality, honesty, integrity. (Merriam-Webster.com, 2011)*
>
> ***Good:*** *Adjective. Of high quality. (Merriam-Webster.com, 2011)*

God says all of His children who remain in Him will grow the fruits of the spirit: love, joy, peace, patience, kindness, goodness, gentleness and self-control. But sometimes we forget and treat each other like spoiled fruit. We forget that we are God's children. It's time to remind yourself of the truth. Let me call out some of the goodness I know about you!

You are bold, loving, and sensible.

"God doesn't want us to be shy with his gifts, but bold and loving and sensible." ~II Timothy 1:7 (the Message)

Your future is going to be great and full of hope.

"For I know the plans I have for you," says the LORD. "They are plans for good and not for disaster, to give you a future and a hope." ~Jeremiah 29:11

You are so dearly loved and nothing, NO THING, can separate you from God's love.

"For I am convinced that neither death nor life, neither angels nor demons, neither the present nor the future, nor any powers, neither height nor depth, nor anything else in all creation, will be able to separate us from the love of God that is in Christ Jesus our Lord." ~Romans 8:38-39

You can do anything with His help.

"I can do all things through Christ who strengthens me." ~Phil. 4:13

You can ask for anything and you will be heard.

"In the morning, LORD, you hear my voice; in the morning I lay my requests before you and wait expectantly." ~Psalm 5:3

You will always have your needs met.

"Look at the birds of the air, that they do not sow, nor reap nor gather into barns, and yet your heavenly Father feeds them. Are you not worth much more than they?" ~Matthew 6:26 (NASB)

You are strong and courageous.

"Have I not commanded you? Be strong and courageous. Do not be frightened, and do not be dismayed, for the Lord your God is with you wherever you go." ~Joshua 1:9 (ESV)

SHE IS UNBROKEN…

List 10 things that are good in your life right now:

1.
2.
3.
4.
5.
6.
7.
8.
9.
10.

Do you struggle with believing some of the statements listed in the previous section are true for you? Why or why not?

What is God saying to you as you complete today's study?

DAY 27:

FINDING GENTLENESS

"Let your gentleness be evident to all. The Lord is near." ~Philippians 4:5

TRUTH STATEMENT®

I choose gentleness.

SHE EMBRACES THE CRACKS...

A bedtime battle was raging. The baby was screaming outside the closed door of her big sister's room. She was banging her little fists and hollering at the top of her lungs for the bottle she should have had 30 minutes ago. Behind that door was a frustrated second grader in the midst of an emotional sensory processing meltdown that had lasted already 40 minutes.

Downstairs, the child in the middle was having a standoff at the dinner table. All I was asking for was five more green beans and three more bites of potato. Hardly a life-or-death situation. He thought so and after repeatedly telling me "No," he was told to sit there until he ate or bedtime, whichever came first. He was hollering "Mommy" at the top of his lungs. I'm all alone during this bedtime brawl.

I'm fighting the urge to lose it completely. But some of the crazy was starting to leak out. I couldn't even help it when I blurted out to the oldest, "You are being selfish. I can't spend any more time on your homework. I have to take care of the baby now." I'm sure my eyes were shooting daggers and I could feel my blood pressure rising.

This was not the kind of bedtime scene I wanted. But, in the land of Mommy-hood, is anything quite like we planned? I can't even count the times I've lost it and acted like the world's worst mommy. Not gentle at all. It's times like this I'm reminded of the verse:

"How gracious God will be when you cry for help! As soon as he hears, he will answer you." ~Isaiah 30:19

I'm so glad God hears the cries of His anxious and overwhelmed daughter. He is quick to rush in with grace, peace, and calmness when I ask. He is much gentler than I am and clearly He can handle crisis with ease. It doesn't have to be any fancier than "HELP!" He knows this life is not easy. He knows my emotions get frazzled, my nerves get raw, and my temper flares. He knows and He loves me anyway. He knows I'm not super mom. He doesn't expect me to be.

What *does He* expect of us? Gentleness, and the ability to ask for help and grace, when we completely blow it. We need to be women who are real, not women who are perfect. We need to admit our mistakes, say we are sorry, and robe ourselves in the beautiful fabric of gentleness. No, I'm not a super mom, but I'm leaning on a super God. And that makes all the difference in the world.

SHE IS DETERMINED...

Years ago, while I was participating in a Bible Study with some women from my small town church, I remember hearing the pastor's wife share her heart about being a "gentle woman." She was lamenting that she never had that quiet and gentle spirit that godly women were supposed to develop. She finally threw up her hands and with a mischievous look on her face said, "It just isn't me!" I remember thinking, *"Amen, sister!"*

Thank you, Jesus, gentleness doesn't equal perfection. No perfect women required in the realm of gentleness! Gentle is something we can all learn to be more of. On the next page you will find a few verses on gentleness in the Bible. As you look up each verse, be sure to write it in the space below. Also jot down any notes on what you are learning about the spirit of gentleness:

- Matthew 11:29-30

- Titus 3:2

- James 3:17

"I choose gentleness… nothing is won by force. I choose to be gentle. If I raise my voice may it be only in praise. If I clench my fist, may it be only in prayer. If I make a demand, may it be only of myself. " ~Max Lucado

SHE IS UNBROKEN...

In your own words, how would you describe gentleness? What does it mean to you to have a gentle spirit?

What characteristic of gentleness do you need to develop more of in your life? How will you do it?

What is God saying to you as you complete today's study?

DAY 28:
FINDING SELF-CONTROL

"Know this, my beloved brothers: let every person be quick to hear, slow to speak, slow to anger; for the anger of man does not produce the righteousness of God." ~James 1:19-20 (ESV)

TRUTH STATEMENT®

My words have power so I will be quick to hear, slow to speak, and slow to anger.

SHE EMBRACES THE CRACKS...

I'm a mom of three littles under the age of 10. Self-control is a daily struggle. And I don't mean for those kids. For me. Learning to control my words is something God and I have been working on forever. The Bible is not silent when it comes to self-control and what I've noticed to be a common struggle for women is the ability to control our tongues. Sweet friend, we must get control of the words we say because we are not reflecting His character when we say whatever we want, whenever we want. We are reflecting something much darker.

> *"For out of the abundance of the heart the mouth speaks. The good person out of his good treasure brings forth good, and the evil person out of his evil treasure brings forth evil. I tell you, on the day of judgment people will give account for every careless word they speak, for by your words you will be justified, and by your words you will be condemned." ~Matthew 12:34-37*

This is serious stuff! EVERY careless word out of our mouths will be judged someday. God wouldn't bother with this warning if He didn't put an enormous amount of importance on the words that come out of our mouths. And let's just get real. The people who live with you and love you the most are usually the ones who are treated the worst when it comes to what you say. Not everything you want to say should be said. We have to learn to choose our words wisely.

Women who are learning to embrace their broken pieces will reflect their healing in how they speak. They will trade in their careless words and instead learn how to build up, encourage, and edify the most important people in their lives. They will listen more than they speak. They will think before they talk. They will get the skills they need to say hard things and resolve conflict with honor. God girls do not fight dirty.

When I started to take seriously the power of my words, and break the bad communication patterns, we were still walking through the worst years of our marriage. It took me years to learn how to develop this skill because I was so broken and bitter… in fact, I distinctly remember biting my cheek all the time in the beginning to keep from saying something sarcastic or snarky (or just plain mean!) when we were in conflict.

If out of the heart the mouth speaks, what is your heart saying? Having an uncontrolled tongue will destroy your life faster than you can imagine. I promise you that your words will make or break you. Take my hand friend, and let's explore what it means to speak with wisdom and self-control.

SHE IS DETERMINED...

Do you find yourself getting angry very quickly at the people you care about the most (spouse, children, friends, parents, etc.) instead of pausing to think before you say something hurtful? I want to tell you that anger is often a "cover-up" emotion for a deeper hurt or need that is not being met. It is usually masking feelings of disappointment, hurt, sadness, and other emotions that are more difficult to deal with (and make you vulnerable). So, instead of dealing with your true feelings, you act with anger.

Communication patterns are largely learned behaviors, so you do have the ability to re-learn bad habits and speak with wisdom and self-control. The Bible talks about the power of your words and controlling your tongue over 100 times in scripture.

Listed below are a few of my favorites that help me remember the importance of controlling my tongue:

"The Lord will fight for you; you need only be still." ~Exodus 14:14

"Whoever keeps his mouth and his tongue keeps himself out of trouble." ~Proverbs 21:23 (ESV)

"Death and life are in the power of the tongue, and those who love it will eat its fruits." ~Proverbs 18:21 (ESV)

"It is better to live in a desert land than with a quarrelsome and fretful woman." ~Proverbs 21:19 (ESV)

"With our tongues we bless God our Father; with the same tongues we curse the very men and women he made in his image. Curses and blessings out of the same mouth! My friends, this can't go on." ~James 3:10-12 (the Message)

SHE IS UNBROKEN…

What is your biggest struggle when it comes to controlling your tongue?

What are some practical ways you can start to change bad communication habits? (ie: pause before you speak harshly, listen more, etc.) What do you need to do to make these changes a reality?

What is God telling you as you complete today's study?

DAY 29:

SHE IS RESOLVED

"But the Lord stood with me and strengthened me." ~2 Timothy 4:17

TRUTH STATEMENT®

I am determined. I am resolved. I will persevere.

SHE EMBRACES THE CRACKS...

In 2003, my young husband and I were fresh off a painful separation period as our moving van crossed the border into a small Western North Dakota town. I was young, broken, unsure, but determined. I wanted our marriage to work more than anything. I needed to move past the horrible things that happened that first year and heal. I was looking for a fresh start; and this little town was going to be my new beginning. I was resolved.

What I found in that little town was not a new beginning. In fact, most of the worst years of our marriage happened in that town. I found myself dealing with things I could never have imagined as we drove that rental truck to our new apartment. The truth is, 22-year-old me had no idea the levels of sadness, anger, mental illness, and toxic behaviors I would reach while I lived in that town. Apparently, rock bottom has a basement.

Less than 45 minutes from that little city where I spent those six horrible years, nestled in gorgeous Theodore Roosevelt National Park, is the tiny town of Medora. Because we lived so close, we spent many hours hiking, camping, and just spending time in this history-rich area. And it's one of my favorite places on earth to this day because it's one of the few spots I have good memories of this time of my life.

Eleven years later, we took our family back to Medora. As we drove out of town on the red gravel road that would take us to that remote area we considered "our spot," I thought about the last time I was there. I was eight and a half months pregnant with our first child. My husband did not think it was wise for me to go because pregnant women shouldn't be hiking in remote areas, obviously. But I didn't want to be left out. I was dealing with my first round of depression while being pregnant and being alone was terrifying.

"Wow. It's been 10 years since I've been back to our spot," I said out loud as we rounded the final corner. I looked around the beautiful countryside and I started to tear up. I realized those two naive broken kids, who found that spot all those years ago, were still in the same truck together. We really had climbed out of rock bottom. The tears flowed as I realized one more broken piece had been mended and one more scar told one more story of an unbroken woman.

SHE IS DETERMINED...

> ***Resolved:*** *Adjective. Fully committed to achieving a goal. (Merriam-Webster.com, 2011)*
>
> ***Determination:*** *Noun. A quality that makes you continue trying to do or achieve something that is difficult. The act of finding out or calculating something. The act of officially deciding something." (Merriam-Webster.com, 2011)*
>
> ***Persevere:*** *Verb. To continue despite difficulties, opposition, or discouragement. (Merriam-Webster.com, 2011)*

Without resolve, determination, and the ability to persevere, I would not have experienced the beautiful restoration of my own brokenness. You simply cannot embrace the broken pieces of your life without resolution, determination, and perseverance.

Sometimes you need a little boost to your resolve. Sometimes you need to be reminded you are a strong determined woman. Let's be real… you need a kick in the perseverance. Take a few moments and look up the following verses, then answer the question that follows.

- Daniel 1:8-9
- Romans 5:3-4
- Hebrews 12:1-3
- James 1:2-4
- 2 Peter 1:5-8

What does the Bible say about being resolved, having determination, and persevering?

SHE IS UNBROKEN...

If you could go back and give the younger version of yourself some advice on how to continue to persevere in spite of the brokenness you will experience, what would you say?

Dear me (age ______)

Love, Me (____________________________sign your name)

What is God saying to you as you complete today's study?

DAY 30:

SHE IS UNBROKEN

"Therefore, if anyone is in Christ, he is a new creation. The old has passed away; behold, the new has come." ~2 Corinthians 5:17

TRUTH STATEMENT®

I am a new creation. I find my true strength in weakness. I am unbroken.

SHE EMBRACES THE CRACKS...

Welcome to Unbroken. As I write the final day of our 30-day journey, I can't help but get a little teary-eyed as I imagine you reaching this day and taking a deep breath and saying, "Wow. I finished." I bet there were times you wanted to give up. I bet there were moments you did not want to dig any deeper for fear you really would break in half. I felt like that sometimes too, even while writing this study. But, you didn't quit. You did the hard work and you are on your way! I'm so proud of you.

You, my friend, are a new creation. Sure you still have the scars where the storms tried to take you out. You still have the memories of hard fought battles and well-earned victories. You might even have some wounds that are not fully healed yet. But you are not broken. Not anymore. You are a new creation. You are stronger, braver, and wiser than you were just 30-days ago. That my friend is priceless.

> *"The strength of a woman is not measured by the impact that all her hardships in life have had on her; but the strength of a woman is measured by the extent of her refusal to allow those hardships to dictate her and who she becomes." ~C. JoyBell C.*

In the 1991 film, *Hook*, the late Robin Williams plays an aging Peter Pan who is suddenly transported back to Neverland because Captain Hook steals his children. The problem is, Peter has completely forgotten how to be Peter Pan. In one of my favorite scenes of all time, the lost boys are fighting over whether or not this old man is even Peter Pan at all. They've drawn battle lines and they are screaming and yelling trying to prove themselves. Out of the crowd, this darling little boy grabs Peter's face and starts looking in his eyes. He moves his wrinkles around and forces him to smile and finally he says, "There you are, Peter!"

I feel like that is where we have landed today, sweet friend. I might not know your name, but I understand your struggle to find true healing and wholeness. I might not know your circumstances, but I know the battle you have bravely fought to embrace the broken pieces of your life. I may not be able to recognize your face in a crowd; but I recognize your soul because it's like our Father's and I can happily say to you, "There you are."

Welcome to Unbroken.
~ Raychel

SHE IS DETERMINED...

> *"So Jacob was left alone, and a man wrestled with him till daybreak. When the man saw that he could not overpower him, he touched the socket of Jacob's hip so that his hip was wrenched as he wrestled with the man. Then the man said, "Let me go, for it is daybreak."*
>
> *But Jacob replied, "I will not let you go unless you bless me." The man asked him, "What is your name?" "Jacob," he answered.*
>
> *Then the man said, "Your name will no longer be Jacob, but Israel, because you have struggled with God and with humans and have overcome." Jacob said, "Please tell me your name."*
>
> *But he replied, "Why do you ask my name?" Then he blessed him there.*

So Jacob called the place Peniel, saying, "It is because I saw God face to face, and yet my life was spared." The sun rose above him as he passed Peniel, and he was limping because of his hip." ~Genesis 32:22-33

We have spent the last month going through a process that would allow you to embrace the broken pieces in your life and find strength and wholeness. Tucked in this passage in Genesis is a beautiful reminder of the journey you have taken. You might not see it right away but let's see how Jacob had a similar experience:

1. **Days 1-7: Choices -** In ancient times, your name identified your character. It was literally a label telling everyone what kind of person you were. Jacob means "deceiver." In verse 27, Jacob comes face to face with his most damaging label.

2. **Days 8-14: Storms & Scars -** In verse 25, we read that Jacob was injured during this encounter with the Angel and would suffer a permanent limp. Just like Jacob, we all bear the scars of our toughest battles.

3. **Days 15-21: Promises, Promises -** In verses 26-28, we see Jacob demanding a blessing from this angel before he will let him go. The angel blesses him with a brand new name and a brand new identity. He was no longer Jacob, but Israel. He now wore the label "overcomer."

4. **Days 22-28: Joy Comes in the Morning -** Jacob wrestled with an angelic creator, whom many scholars argue was God Himself, and didn't die. He was hurt but he won the victory! He earned the blessing because he didn't give up and in the morning, when the dust settled and all was said and done, he praised God.

SHE IS UNBROKEN...

How did you feel when you read about Jacob wrestling with God and how it closely parallels what you have learned in this study?

As you reflect over the last 30 days, what has been your biggest "Ah-ha" moment or take away?

What is God saying to you as you complete today's study?

FIVE YEARS LATER:
THE PLOT TWIST

"And I will bring my people back from exile. "They will rebuild the ruined cities and live in them. They will plant vineyards and drink their wine; they will make gardens and eat their fruit. I will plant Israel in their own land, never again to be uprooted from the land I have given them." Says the Lord your God." ~Amos 9:14-15

On October 18, 2017, my divorce was final. The marriage I had prayed so hard for God to restore was over and my life was a giant pile of ashes. I wanted a redemption story. A love story for the ages. Not more brokenness. I felt like God broke his promise to me by not restoring our marriage.

Looking back the promise was not to restore the broken marriage. The promise was to take care of me and the kids, no matter what, if I got out of the way. Nearly 12 years later, I see that promise fulfilled. I got the restoration I was praying for. And God has protected us every step of the way.

In 15th century Japan a Japanese shogun broke a favorite tea bowl and sent it back to China to be fixed. But the repair job, which was done with metal staples – being the standard for repair at that time – detracted from the beauty of the bowl.

Disappointed, the shogun enlisted a Japanese craftsman to come up with a more aesthetically pleasing solution, and kintsugi was born.

Kintsugi is the Japanese art of repairing broken pottery with lacquer dusted or mixed with powdered gold, silver, or platinum. As a philosophy, it treats breakage and repair as part of the history of an object, rather than something to disguise.

A few years ago, God whispered some encouragement to my broken heart, "Look up. Your story is bigger than your first marriage. Your harvest is full." And what I saw was not just a field all full of weeds with the sloughs running amuck called "The Wastelands," I saw acres of possibilities and new growth.

The redemption story I wanted was my first marriage. The redemption story I got was my own. The cracks and broken pieces of my life have been strengthened with the gold and silver of wisdom and resilience. And my life is more beautiful than I ever expected. I am still, and always will be, unbroken.

~Raychel

ACKNOWLEDGEMENTS

Thank you, Jesus, for healing broken pieces and creating a masterpiece from the mess.

To Bugs, Baby Man, and Tootie - it's not easy when mommy is a writer and on a tight deadline. You three were champs! Thanks for stepping up and pitching in so mom could get this book written. Love you to the moon and back.

To the participants of the *UNBROKEN* Faith Coaching Experience - my Unbroken Warriors! You were the first to read my words, the first to embrace this message with love and acceptance, the first to answer the tough questions, and the first to blaze a brand new trail towards healing and restoration. Thank you is hardly sufficient. You're courage, tenacity, and tenderness will not be forgotten.

To the ones that caused some of the deepest wounds in my heart - this one's for you.

WORKS

(n.d.). Retrieved from Wikipedia: https://en.wikipedia.org/wiki/Viktor_Frankl

(n.d.). Retrieved from Postpartum Progress: www.postpartumprogress.org Church, U. C.

(n.d.). Catechism of the Catholic Church. Dillion, S.

(n.d.). 7 Ways to Deal with Change. Retrieved from www.lifeways.org. Edward W. Goodrick, J. R. (2004).

The Strongest NIV Exhaustive Concordance . Zondervan . Kendrick, A. (2013).

The Love Dare. B&H Books. Merriam-Webster.com. (2011). Retrieved May - July 2016

Anderson, M. (2016, second edition 2021) She Who Overcomes. RAYMA Team, LLC.

Nietzsche, F. (1997). Twilight of the Idols. Hackett Publishing Company. Sterne, L. (1760). Sermons, Vol. 1 Number 12

ABOUT THE AUTHOR

Raychel Perman is a Certified Life Coach, Business Coach, Speaker, Author, and Co-Founder of RAYMA Team, LLC. She is the Co-host of the She Who Overcomes™ Podcast and is funny, wise, and tells it like it is. Raychel shares her story of overcoming trauma and living with mental health challenges to inspire others to believe that the broken pieces of their past can lead to beauty, strength, and new beginnings.

Raychel has a Bachelor of Science in Psychology and Christian Counseling from Liberty University. She is a licensed Esthetician with over two decades of experience in the beauty industry. Raychel, her husband Josh, and her three children make their home in North Dakota. Connect with her at www.raychelperman.com.

Made in the USA
Columbia, SC
22 January 2023

10086246R00109